Is There a Family in the House?

Is There a Family in the House?

A Realistic and Hopeful Look
at Marriage and the Family Today

Kenneth Chafin

WORD BOOKS
PUBLISHER
WACO, TEXAS

This book is dedicated to my wife

BARBARA BURKE CHAFIN

who after twenty-four years of marriage
is an increasingly interesting person,
a very exciting partner,
and a devoted mother

Acknowledgments

The people whose involvement in my life has contributed to the understanding reflected in this book live in many places in this land and span a fifty-year period. The process of writing the book renewed my sense of gratitude for them. They are joined by a host of family and friends whose interest and encouragement have nourished me.

A number of associates and friends have helped. Three colleagues on our staff—Bob Hines, Dick Stafford, and Betty Thomas—read the early drafts and made helpful suggestions. Betty conducted the children's survey which is reported in chapter 7. Yvonne Garrett, a homemaker and for several years teacher of classes in marriage enrichment, spent time with me discussing parenting and the roles of mothers today.

I am especially grateful to Linda Blevins Jones for ideas she shared concerning the structure of the book, for books she loaned me that helped in additional research, and for invaluable suggestions she made. But I am most indebted for her interest and encouragement, the time she devoted and the energy she expended as throughout the process I was able to call on her for evaluation, reactions, and suggestions.

In spite of all the helpers listed above the book wouldn't have made it to press except for three people. My secretary, Doris Estes, did part of the typing and orchestrated the whole process which sent the chapters to the publisher. Jane Mahns did the original transcription from tape and ten months later did most of the final draft. That first draft was edited for me by Barbara McNeir. Without her work I probably would never have sent it to a publisher.

Everything we did was made more readable by the editors. I'm indebted to Floyd Thatcher for his patience, to Al Bryant for his skill, and to Mary Ruth Howes for all her helpfulness.

Contents

Introduction

This book is the result of a concern for the family that has been growing in me for several years. Events which have happened around me have forced me to an increased awareness of what our society and its pressures are doing to the family. Being in a family and living in an intimate relationship with hundreds of families as a pastor has created in me both a greater appreciation for the family and a greater concern.

More than a year ago I came to the conclusion that for the next several years of my life I would focus my attention on the family. As a way of giving visibility to that commitment, last year on the six Sundays between Mother's Day and Father's Day I presented a series of sermons on the different aspects of marriage and the family. The number of persons who expressed appreciation for my encouraging words about the family simply confirmed my feeling that people were seeking help with their marriages and their families. That experience led to the writing of this book.

My perspective in the book is primarily that of a husband and father. Yet I have also been affected in my thinking by some of the healthy, effective families I'm constantly in contact with in the church. The book is not primarily the result of research done but the sharing of life lived and observed.

The process of writing the book has been for me a spiritual experience. Always as I wrote there was an awareness of my marriage of twenty-four years with Barbara and my role as parent to two teenagers and one grown daughter. During this time there has been born in me a desire to make more of my marriage and my family. I pray you may have the same experience as you read the book.

As you read you will discover that I am realistic about life and hopeful about the family. The family is the most important and most enduring institution in our society. When you realize that it's composed of a man and a woman who marry and the children born of that union it seems rather fragile. But what happens in that marriage relationship and in that family will determine what kind of people will live in this world.

The book is positive and helpful. It's written for the young and old. Wherever you are with your family you will be able to relate. A single adult would find it excellent preparation for marriage.

More than anything else I'd like for the book to heighten your awareness of what it takes to make a good marriage and an effective family and to encourage you to think about your own family, where it is and where you would like it to go.

KENNETH CHAFIN

Is There a Family in the House?

1

Pictures of the Family

Society's most important institution is the family. Like so many people I've been guilty of either overlooking or underestimating its importance.

My parents were both the youngest children from two large farm families which had moved from Arkansas to the Cherokee Strip in northeast Oklahoma while they were still children. While still in their teens they married and began their family during one of the most difficult economic depressions this nation has ever suffered. Into this family were born two boys and two girls. I am the oldest child. When the youngest was born my parents could no longer make a living on the small farm so we moved to the Quad Cities in northern Illinois where both of my parents took jobs in industry.

My father worked with the furnaces at International Harvester and hardened the gears which went into tractors. My mother was a seamstress who did piecework in a clothing factory. Both jobs were physically and emotionally demanding, involved long hours, and they earned just enough money to provide for the necessities of life.

It must have been a time of great pressure and stress for both of them as they sought to bring up their children in a different kind of world from the one in which they had been reared. I'm equally sure that they must have felt quite inadequate as they addressed themselves to the task of preparing their children for life. Yet as I think of my parents, I'm amazed at what they were able to do with so little help and under such difficult circumstances. They developed our thinking and shaped our attitudes and equipped us for living. Whatever our family may have lacked it was the most important influence in my life.

I think that many of us marry and begin our families without fully realizing the key role the family can play both for us and for society. There are a number of reasons for this. We have all been influenced too much by those who have made a vocation of debunking marriage and the family. Several years ago I was preparing a lecture on the family. Anxious to do some more reading on the subject, I dropped by the bookstore and purchased a number of books which focused on some aspects of the family. To my shock and surprise three of the five books operated from the assumption that the family was an "over-the-hill" institution and that the sooner we could come up with a viable alternative the better off we would be. Television is equally at fault. It is extremely difficult for couples to develop an awareness of the importance of the family at the same time they are constantly exposed to caricatures of the family in the media.

It is also possible to spend so much time and energy focusing on the weaknesses in the family that we fail to recognize its legitimate strengths. It is one of the sad characteristics of our human nature that the things which go wrong often get more of our attention than the things which go right. As a result the news covers the employee who embezzled and not the honest persons, the family who had a wreck and not the ones who arrived safely, and the juveniles who robbed a store and not those who didn't. Knowing that this is the way we are, before we come to any conclusion about the role of the family we need to give some attention to its positive aspects.

Our growing overdependence upon the other institutions in our society tends to undermine the family. General education has been taken over by the schools, and the family has less and less input into the process. Religious education seems to have been turned over to the church with parents feeling less and less responsibility. There is an increased tendency to look to the government to provide services which have been traditionally provided by the family. All this has tended to blind us to the real importance of the family in our world. While school, church, and government may be allies of the family, they can never be substitutes for it.

If the family fails then all the other institutions of society will fail. The family is that basic unit of society which undergirds all else. Every influence which weakens the family and makes it more difficult for it to do its job will ultimately weaken society. All that is done to build strong, healthy, happy, and effective families will increase the possibility of a strong and healthy society. Any effort to deal with the problems we face without dealing with their roots within the family is short-sighted.

Daily we are made aware of the debates going on in the United Nations and the effect they could have upon our lives. We read of hearings before congressional committees and see that we citizens are involved. Press releases from the White House that change things for us have become commonplace. But we need to become aware that the future of the country is being settled not by ambassadors, congressmen, or presidents —but by parents. The building of an effective, healthy family unit is the most important business in the world.

The family is a universal phenomenon. It is the institution which not only permits survival but prepares children for life. Compared to the length of man's history, the interest of the social scientists in the study of the family has been rather recent. But long before we developed those skills which allow us to understand better the inner workings of the family the Bible pictured the family as of primary importance. It was not by accident that the book of beginnings (Genesis) starts with the first family and lays the foundation for the character and purpose of Israel in the experiences and understanding which the families of Abraham, Isaac, and Jacob had with God.

When God came to reveal himself to us most perfectly in his own Son, he came as a little baby into a family. And even a casual reading of Christ's teachings and ministry will reveal how aware he was of the family and how interested he was in it. When he attempted to describe in parable form how God feels about us he told the story of a family in which there were two sons. We know it as the story of the "prodigal son." Recently we've been taught to think of it as the parable of the "waiting father."

A Family Is . . .

Even when we have agreed on the importance of the family, there is need to define just what we mean when we say "family." This need was dramatized for me recently as I sat talking to a close friend whose husband was killed in an accident several years ago. She said, "I don't think you've made clear what you mean by family. For instance, am I a family? Or do I have to have a husband? Or, if I had a child would I be a family?"

The question was a gentle reminder that we all tend to use the word family as though we were always speaking of a father, a mother, and children. While the overall context of this book pictures the basic family as having two parents and children, I am acutely aware that there are many families where this is not the pattern.

My first real awareness of the deep need for help in the single-parent family came when several years ago I began work with a significant number of single adults. I had not been with them long until I became aware that at least a third of them had been married and had children from that marriage for whom they now bore the major responsibility. There was a time when all of these single-parent families would have been headed by women, but this is no longer the case. I'm seeing an increasing number of men who are functioning as the only parent. While this is a difficult role to play it isn't impossible, and I am witness to many single-parent families which, with a little help, are doing a good job. There will be a special section in the chapter on parenting relating to some specific helps for this type of family.

The "blended family" is a new family formed from former families. This can create the "his, hers, and ours" kind of situation with children and an infinitely complex set of relationships. The "part-time" family deals with the parent who has custody of the children on weekends and possibly during school vacation time.

While his/her time is limited with the children this parent wants the family to accomplish good in the lives of those involved.

There are many variations of what is considered the traditional family unit. Each has a specific set of opportunities and problems. There are a growing number of excellent books which address themselves to these kinds of families. But whatever the makeup of your family you will find certain needs and emphases are held in common by all of them.

One of the best ways to recognize the importance of the family is to remember what the family is designed to do. The Continental Congress on the Family was held during the past decade and was one of the most significant meetings in America. It brought together writers and speakers who were experts in their fields, Christian in their orientation, and both helpful and hopeful in their approach to the family. From this congress has come some of the most helpful material in pointing out what Christian families especially can do to deepen the ties and strengthen the spiritual dimensions of the home.

Edith Schaeffer, wife of the distinguished theologian-author Dr. Francis Schaeffer, brought a paper on "What Is a Family?" Instead of involving herself in endless and complicated definitions she gave some graphic "pictures" of the family. I identified with the word pictures of the family which Edith Schaeffer used and they called forth a host of vivid images. I'm indebted to her for being a catalyst to my thought about the family.

A Place to Grow People

The family is a balanced environment designed by God for the growth of human beings. I recall a certain sense of alarm when several years ago I heard a scientist discuss how very fragile the environment for life is upon the earth. This scientist pointed out that there is just a thin crust on which things can be grown and a relatively thin layer of atmosphere which will support life. He said that comparatively speaking it was like the thin shell of an egg.

Some of the most wholesome and helpful movies and television programs made are those which give us a better understanding of all the forms of life on our planet and the ways in which they relate to one another. When we were first married, Barbara and I went to see Walt Disney's "Living Desert." I had lived in the west but was almost totally unaware of the abundance of life in the desert. God's provision for each form of life there astonished me.

I have a niece who is a very talented young wild-life artist. She personifies for me the whole new awareness of the importance of ecological balance. When she comes to visit us it's fun to let her show me my own back yard. Not only does she know the names of what she sees, but she knows the ways in which they relate to one another. She still lives at home with my sister in that part of south Texas usually referred to as "the valley." You would be fascinated with their yard. They have worked hard to create the kind of environment in which unusual frogs, beautiful butterflies, and rare tropical birds will live and grow. My niece has succeeded to the degree that she now has forms of life in her yard rarely seen in her area.

Human beings need that same kind of balanced family environment in which to develop. As a child, one of the first verses I memorized from the Bible was, "Jesus increased in wisdom and stature, and in favor with God and man" (KJV). This is a description of the balanced growth he experienced in the human family in which God placed him. His body developed. His mind grew. He developed socially, and he grew spiritually. This is the kind of development which each of us wants for his children. At the same time we are aware of the delicate balance which is required.

Howard and Sarah Lee are friends who have a small ranch about an hour's drive from Houston. On the ranch are several ponds and one small lake of several acres. The lake is full of all sorts of fish—crappie, catfish, bream, and bass. I have a standing invitation to fish in the lake and try to take advantage of it as often as my schedule will allow. My son and I love to catch those large bream on a light flyrod. Before my father passed away, we would always go fishing together there when he visited me. Over the past several years Howard noticed that while the lake was full of bass they seemed to stop growing when they reached about ten inches in length.

The Lees are city people so they draw upon the experience of their country neighbors when something occurs that they don't understand. So Howard went down to the local store and asked Gus, who along with many other good qualities, is the local expert on ponds. Upon hearing the description of what was happening he surmised, "It sounds to me like your lake is out of balance. Those bass will never get as big as they ought to until you get the lake balanced. Get the county agent down here to test it and tell you what to do." Even a fish (which will end up as a stuffed trophy on someone's wall, or better yet, a high protein meal on someone's table) needs a certain kind of environment.

While the family is infinitely more complex, the picture is essentially the same. A proper blending of the roles of father and mother is required. There needs to be a balance between dependence and independence. Freedom and responsibility need to live in a healthy tension. A family takes energy, interest, commitment, love, and a lot of hard work—but it is more than worth it all because people made in the image of God need just the right kind of environment in which to develop to their full potential. And while there is no friendly "county agent" whom you can call to make scientific studies of the "unbalance" in your family and prescribe a sure cure, there is a great deal which you and I *can* learn and do to assist us in the building of this climate for healthy growth.

A Center for Creativity

The family is the most important center for the development of creativity there is. This is where self-trust, which is at the heart of all creativity, is first nurtured. In the family the discipline is developed which frees persons to be truly creative. The family provides the fertile soil in which individual gifts and interest are encouraged to develop and mature. We need to see this picture of the family as a creative center.

I wish you could meet my Aunt Alice. She's now past seventy. When she was a child in the home somehow a shotgun accidentally discharged, hitting her. As a result she has worn an artificial limb since she was a teenager. This did not keep her from marrying and having a family. Uncle Milton taught school and Aunt Alice gave herself to homemaking with energy left over for community, church, and neighbors. People sort of felt sorry for Aunt Alice because she had so little, worked so hard, and couldn't get around as well as others. But one of the fond memories of my life is a day spent with her family more than forty years ago.

The little house which was perched on the banks of

a small creek barely protected the family from the elements and had no modern conveniences. The yard was an interesting assortment of flowers, shrubs, kittens, puppies, and chickens. It looked like a scene out of John Steinbeck's *Grapes of Wrath*.

We had hardly arrived when it began to shower. This meant that suddenly two families of children who had looked forward to playing together were cooped up in the house. Though I'm sure she had other things to do with her time, Aunt Alice felt that we children needed something interesting to do. So she found the instructions for making play dough which she had saved from one of the farm magazines (this was years before anyone considered the commercial manufacture of it). To keep the dough from being the color of the flour which was its main ingredient she colored it with bluing. She gathered all of us around the table and initiated a contest to see which child could form the most interesting animal.

By noon, the sun had come out and burned off the overcast so all the children decided to go fishing in the creek. It didn't take us long to discover that all the fish were gone from the creek but that it was full of large crawdads. (I later was told that the proper name was crayfish.) We soon filled a milking pail with them. When we took them to the house one of Aunt Alice's boys asked, "Mother, have you ever tasted a crawdad tail?" Without so much as batting an eye she replied, "No, but I think it would be interesting." She showed us how to clean them, then she salted them, rolled them in meal, and fried them a crispy brown. I can still remember the sense of adventure experienced by the whole group as we gathered around her table to eat something none of us had ever tasted before.

All of Aunt Alice's children are now married, of

course, and they have grown children of their own. During the past several years I've had a chance to be with them on several occasions. They are all happy, whole people with wonderful children. I have a feeling that the foundation for their lives was being laid when they lived in the little house on the creek-bank. That family was a hotbed of creativity.

God designed the family to be a liberating force in our lives.

A Place of Safety and Security

One of the most beautiful and meaningful pictures of the family is as a shelter from the storms of life. Life does have its storms for each of us and the family not only provides us with a place of shelter during these storms, but the family can actually be drawn closer together in the process of providing security for each other.

Those of us who are older may have forgotten what a storm looks like to a small child. Children want to climb every tree, and run down every hill, but if they fall and skin a knee they need a place to flee to and a person who will comfort them and make them feel safe. A child needs to feel the hands and arms of those who love him and hear the soothing words of those who care. The little child learns early that the family is a kind of sanctuary to which he can flee when storm clouds loom.

For a young child the storm may be the loss of a pet. Our son had a little beagle pup whom he named Spitfire. That pup was a bundle of energy and a source of delight to everyone—but especially to Troy. One day I came home to discover that Spitfire was dead. He had been playing under a car whose driver did not see him and he had been killed when the driver drove off.

I went back to Troy's room where he was sitting on the edge of his bed crying. Sitting down beside him, I put my arms around him and held him while he wept over the loss of his puppy. He was too young to be introduced to the process of grief without feeling the love and sympathy and security of his family.

If you have teenagers in your home you probably wonder if they look upon the family as a shelter. It seems that teenagers are seldom at home and if given a choice would rather be with their friends than with their family. When they're home they seem to spend more time in their room than with the rest of the family. Don't let this fool you. Even as they are becoming more independent there is still that need for the familiar objects, familiar people, and familiar routines. They need the family as a place from which to go and to which they can return. And, interestingly enough, they need someone who is really interested to whom they can report.

Even now I find myself drawing comfort from my family during difficult times. Adults do have difficult times. I sat with a man who had been caught in some company reorganization and was suddenly without a job, after working with the same company for more than twenty-five years. Though he was a man of real ability he was shaken. I can still hear him saying, "If it weren't for the support I'm feeling from my family I think this experience would sink me." There is nothing stronger than the love, concern, and support that a family can give its members.

For some reason I have never been afraid of stormy weather. On the contrary I have often found a storm invigorating. When I was a child we lived in a house with a tin roof. My bed was in the attic. I could lie on my back and see the ends of the nails which held the large sheets of galvanized tin to the rafters. I can still remember lying there during a violent storm feeling dry, warm, secure, and safe. I think this is one of the reasons God has given us families. When there are illnesses, or reversals, or disappointments, whether we are young or old, we have a place and people where we can feel loved, accepted, and secure.

A Transmitter of Values

One of the finest pictures of the family is that of a unit which transmits values from generation to generation. As a young schoolboy I became interested in track meets. I once fancied myself as having great potential as a distance runner. Even as a spectator today I find myself fascinated by the one-mile run. But one of the most interesting races at a meet is the relay. It involves teamwork because it combines the talents of four participants. The critical time isn't when the person is running along by himself, though this is important. The most critical time is when one runner races alongside the next runner and hands him the baton. If the pass is clumsy or the baton is dropped it usually means losing the race.

One of the most important truths we can pass on to our children is the fact that people are more important than things. The best place for learning how to treat people is in the home where there is an opportunity to act out love in the situations of life day by day. Here is where respect for life, others, and self is either born or destroyed. There has been a stress upon individualism in our country from its very beginning. Today many persons are translating that into the doctrine of "happiness for myself whatever the cost to others." In the home we learn to think of ourselves as being a part of a family, as being part of something beyond ourselves.

For our family we have found help in what the Scriptures teach about relationships in the home. One of the finest treatises concerning the basis upon which people are to relate to each other was written by the apostle Paul late in the first century (Eph. 5:21–6:4). The passage is brief, less than 300 words. Paul makes no effort to stress everything. But he maintains that the key ingredient in all human relationships is self-giving love. The apostle describes love not just as a feeling but as having to do with choices and actions. Defining love as wanting what is best for the other person whatever the cost to ourselves, he uses as the model God's love for us which was revealed in Christ's sacrifice. The idea of loving others as we have been loved is the motivation. In stark contrast to the definition many people have of love as being weak, sentimental, and ineffective this kind of love is strong, realistic, and gutsy.

This kind of love needs to be acted out in the day-by-day relationships of the family. All of us need to envision the good of others and not always be concerned about our own interests.

Closely related to the idea of the worth of persons is the conveying of moral and spiritual values to a following generation. I was a professor in a seminary during that period when the most fashionable avocation was reacting against all the institutions of society. During this period most of my students were suspicious of nearly everything associated with the establishment, and even though they were preparing for vocational service in the church they had real doubts about her. One day I had as a guest lecturer a man who was a

pastor of a strong congregation. He spoke rather posi-
tively about the role of the church in society and then
gave an opportunity for questions. What he received
instead was a statement.

An angry young man stood and announced, "I appreciate your viewpoint but I do not share it. From
where I stand the church looks like the old gray mare."

This little bit of dialogue attracted everyone's un-
divided attention—including mine! Without the slightest bit of defensiveness the guest lecturer quietly
replied, "I agree with you. Sometimes she looks like the
old gray mare to me too. But what I want you to realize
is that this old gray mare is one of the few institutions
in our world which is going to pass along to the next
generation those values that, when lived by, make life
more worthwhile."

While I look to the church as my ally in passing
along moral and spiritual values, I see the family as
having a better opportunity for success. It is always a
joy to watch the values of one generation being taken
on by the next. This is a source of great joy to parents.
One of the apostle Paul's favorite "sons" in his ministry
was a young man named Timothy. When Paul wrote to
him he stated, "I am reminded of the sincerity of your
faith, a faith which was alive in Lois your grandmother
and Eunice your mother before you, and which, I am
confident, lives in you also" (2 Tim. 1:5). Paul was
describing a faith which remained fresh and vital generation after generation. This is a more complicated
process than passing along a family heirloom to the
children—but it is also infinitely more rewarding.

I believe it is good for us to reaffirm the family. We
need to hang on the walls of our consciousness pictures
which remind us of the purpose of the family in our
lives and in society.

In spite of all the problems we face in society, if all goes well in the family then life is worth living.

A Place with No Problems?

There is one picture you must not get of the family: perfection. It is not a place without problems. There are no perfect families, nor are there any families without problems. Many of the problems are quite predictable. They are built into the complex nature of the relationship of marriage and the family. Everyone who marries, has children, and faces life from the perspective of the family has more or less the same challenges.

These are as much a part of life as having pimples when you're a teenager. They can be looked at and faced and growth can take place in the process.

But there are problems which the family is encountering from society as a whole which create difficulties for the family. Some of these are subtle but some are simply open challenges. In our society we are developing certain destructive attitudes about the family. Our families are constantly being bombarded with evil ideas. There are major revolutions taking place in how people see themselves. These need to be recognized and dealt with if the family is to survive and live up to its potential.

The next chapter will deal with some of the problems we must face.

For further thinking and discussion:

1. What one ideal or value would you most like to pass along to your children?
2. When you were a small child of five or less what did you associate with safety and security in your family? When you were eight? When you were a teenager?
3. How many families do you know which have a

variation of the basic husband and wife and children born of that marriage?

4. What were some of the things you knew your parents would not allow?

5. What ingredients do you think make a family a balanced environment for the developing of people?

2

Problems Each Family Faces

Several years ago Barbara and I were invited to lead a session during a marriage enrichment retreat. This was the first meeting of this sort either of us had ever attended whether as participants or leaders. It was held at a conference center about a hundred miles from Houston. The participants were twenty young couples most of whom had been married five years or less.

We had been married twenty years at the time of the retreat. Instead of making a formal presentation on marriage we were asked simply to talk to these couples about our marriage. The setting was informal which made sharing seem easy and natural. Barbara and I told about the families we were reared in, how we met, what we liked about each other, the wedding, things which surprised us about marriage, differences we still have, the coming of children, and a score of other matters. We took turns, often giving two different versions of the same event. As far as possible, we tried to be open and honest about our relationship.

In the question and answer session which followed,

the young couples registered surprise about two things. First, they were surprised that the kinds of problems we talked about having when we first married were the same ones they were having. Somehow, each of the couples had come to the retreat feeling that what they were going through was almost unique. One of the affirmations they received was the discovery that many of the stresses they were feeling were perfectly normal. Everyone had them. They could be dealt with.

The second surprise was that after twenty years of a good marriage there would still be areas of stress and tension. As I listened to their discussion I received this impression: they had the idea that when a couple married they were delivered a set of problems. Once they dealt with this first set, all would be peaceful and tranquil. What they were failing to grasp was that at each stage of life there arise new situations each of which can present its own crisis to be solved or at least managed. This discovery offers a real opportunity for growth.

One of the most persistent myths in our society is that the normal and healthy family does not experience problems and stress. This myth remains despite the fact that every significant study of the family demonstrates the normal family does not always live in perfect harmony, does get ruffled at times, and does not always cooperate with one another. The difference between the healthy and the destructive family is not the absence of problems but how those problems are seen and dealt with.

If all the problems a family must face were brought together we could organize them into two groups. The first group includes those which grow out of the normal life cycle of the family as it moves from marriage to parenthood to the departure of the children from the home to retirement. Each of these stages has its own problems and its own opportunities. And there are resources for working through each stage in such a way as to bring a sense of fulfillment.

The second set of problems does not arrive from within the family process but from the larger society of which the family is a part. Tremendous social pressures are being brought to bear upon the family. When the American family moved from an essentially rural to an urban life style it created problems for itself never before encountered. Rapid and radical social change is taking place. Ways of living that once were called Bohemian are now being suggested as alternate life styles for us all. There is no place to run from these pressures; we must confront them.

One of the best investments a person can make in his marriage and family is to look realistically at those problems the family must face from within and from without.

The Newlyweds

Often a couple in love does more planning for the wedding than they do for the marriage which is to follow—even though the wedding lasts no more than thirty minutes and the marriage is for a lifetime. But it doesn't take long for both partners to realize that these early days of marriage are going to be full of both excitement and challenge. During this early period before children are born is the time to form strong marital bonds. This is a time for learning how to share each other's lives. During this period there are several tasks which need to be faced. If they aren't confronted and controlled problems will follow.

The first task is learning to make mutual accommodations to each other in large and small routines. Barbara

and I were both in our mid-twenties when we met. We
had both been on our own for several years. I was still
in graduate school but well into my career. So we did
not have to face a lot of questions before we announced
our engagement and plans to marry. We loved each
other, enjoyed each other, understood each other, and
spent literally hours talking about what we wanted
from our life together.

We were married on a warm July afternoon in her
home church in Albany, Georgia. After a brief honeymoon in the Atlantic coast town of Fernandina Beach,
Florida, we moved into the furnished apartment we
had rented near the seminary campus in Ft. Worth.
This is the period when we began to discover all the
little differences in each other that somehow had not
surfaced in those endless hours of late-night talking.

One of the first little spats I remember had to do
with what I ate for breakfast. The first morning in the
apartment she told me that when her mother had left-
over biscuits she would split them, place a slice of
cheese on each half, and toast them in the oven. I had
the feeling that in her family this had been a very
special kind of breakfast, so when she asked if I would
like to try it, I readily agreed. It wasn't bad, but it
wasn't all that enjoyable for me. The second morning
we had the same thing. When the cheese biscuits came
out on the third morning I asked, "Barbara, don't you
know how to fix anything else?"

My question didn't exactly help breakfast that morning! In the little discussion which followed I learned
that for as long as she could remember her father had
never varied his breakfast menu. He liked an egg, toast,
bacon, juice, and coffee. He never varied. When I
seemed to like the cheese biscuits, she thought she had
discovered what I preferred for breakfast. She was set-

tling in to fix them for me throughout our marriage! After twenty-four years I'm still experimenting with breakfast and she's still adjusting to the fact that in this way I'm different from her dad.

Any couple could make a long list of the many areas where they differ. One squeezes the toothpaste tube; the other is a roller. One plans ahead; the other is more spontaneous. One may be more wide awake at night; the other enjoys the morning hours. One is by habit neat; and the other may tend to be messy. Looking back on those times, Barbara and I laugh at how very naive we were about each other. How important those days of adjustments were in building our marriage.

Communication Is Important

A second task during this period is the development of communication styles. The young couple sitting in my office talking about getting married has the opinion that about all they have to do to communicate is hold hands and look into each other's eyes. While this euphoria is a nice feeling it doesn't contribute too much to the planning of the wedding and the reception. It will certainly not replace the need to develop methods which allow the marital pair to understand what is being said, what is being felt, and what is being done.

During college I took courses in communication. At the time we married I had already accumulated ten years of experience in public speaking. Barbara was an experienced writer and editor. Our backgrounds had developed in both of us an awareness of the need to be clear in expression. Though we never actually said it we were of the opinion that we were probably one couple who would have little trouble communicating. Yet during this early period of our marriage we were both constantly being reminded of all the things in our backgrounds and experience which hindered our understanding of each other's words and actions.

In the fall after our marriage the previous summer, Barbara bought a small half-of-ham. With the budget on which we were surviving then, "half a ham" was a luxury. She baked it and we had one of those nice Sunday-type dinners. Then we made some ham sandwiches. Later we sizzled little slivers of it with breakfast. Finally there was nothing left of that ham but the bone. I had a suggestion.

"Barbara," I said, "do you know what my mother would do with a bone like that?" That's probably not the most diplomatically worded question a groom ever asked his bride.

"No. What would your mother do with this bone?" she asked.

"My mother would cook it all day in a big pot of beans and would make a big pan of cornbread to go with it."

"That's exactly what my mother would do," Barbara exclaimed. So plans were made for us to have hambone and beans with cornbread the next night for supper. I could hardly wait.

The next morning as I left for school I reminded her not to forget the beans. She assured me that it was the first thing on her agenda after I left. All day long I could just imagine what our little apartment must smell like with the aroma of those beans simmering on the stove.

When I walked into our apartment that night I knew something had gone wrong. It didn't smell right. I marched to the stove, lifted the lid on the bean pot, and was horrified at what I saw.

Sensing that I wasn't too happy, Barbara asked what

was wrong. A little too much of my disappointment made its way into my voice as I almost shouted, "Where I'm from when they say beans they mean pinto beans." By now she was angry and hurt, and a bit confused at my reaction. So her reply matched mine in volume and sting. "Where I come from," she shouted, "when they say beans they mean green beans."

It only took a minute for both of us to realize how ridiculous we sounded. So we sat down and laughed about the breakdown in communication between a person reared in Georgia and one reared in Oklahoma. Those differing cultures had to be taken into consideration when we were trying to communicate.

The issue of "green beans" or "pintos" is not all that important. But what if our discussion had been about goals for our marriage, roles within the marriage, how we felt about my career, the rearing of children, or religion in the family?

During the past decade I have had occasion to read the books of, listen to lectures by, or have personal conversations with a number of the prominent marriage and family therapists in the country. I am not at all surprised to discover that many of them feel a lack of real communication is one of the major causes of breakdowns in marriages in our country. These first years of the marriage present a good time to begin this helpful process of communication.

From "Me" to "Us"

A third task during this period of marriage is to shift the loyalties from the family in which you were reared to the one you are establishing. When Jesus said, "For this reason a man shall leave his father and mother," he was describing both a painful and a very essential experience. While the exclusive nature of the commitment a husband and wife make to each other will be discussed in the chapter on getting ready for marriage, we need to realize that this is the time in the marriage for that shift to take place. A man or woman who is not equipped to leave the parental home both physically and emotionally can never build a strong marriage. And parents who will not "release" their children cripple their chances for a good marriage.

These first years can be good years if they are used to strengthen the marital ties. This is an especially good time to find an adult expression for your faith and to put down roots of your own. It is a good time to begin extending your family by developing meaningful friendships with other couples who have the same values for their lives and the same goals for their marriage that you have. This is a good time to loosen your ties with those persons, places, and activities which would distract from your marriage. The stronger the marriage becomes during this period the more prepared you will be for parenthood.

It's a Boy/Girl!

Becoming a parent is a most memorable event. Although I have forgotten certain things which happened last week, I can still remember in the most minute detail almost everything that happened from the moment when Barbara announced to me that it was "time" until her mother arrived to help take care of our firstborn. It had not been an easy pregnancy for Barbara and we were so thankful that everything had gone well.

Nancy's birth introduced us to a whole new dimension of family life—parenthood. It marked that period in the marriage when there would be children in the home. This period begins with the birth of the first child and ends when the last one leaves home. It could last as long as thirty years.

Our experience has been that each of our three children has enriched both our marriage and our family. In the light of our experience I find it difficult to identify with the idea which has been given so much expression lately: that children are nice but need to be thought of as interrupting the parents' plans for their own lives. I was taken aback at the suggestion of one social scientist. He said that rather than children fulfilling a marriage they may be the first point of cleavage which separates husband and wife.

For Barbara and me each additional child has been like adding another row of numbers on a calculator. The coming of each child has added an infinite number of relationships to the family. We feel that our children rather than threatening our relationship have strengthened it.

Later, an entire chapter will be devoted to parenting. But here it is important to note that each stage the child goes through creates a new family situation and the potential for a crisis. It also creates the possibility for growth in the relationship. Being married and having children, and being sensitive to change should keep life from ever being dull or commonplace.

One of the most difficult ideas to accept during parenting is that you are preparing your children to leave you. Probably every parent has had our experience with a small child. In the midst of some happy experience where child and parent feel especially close, the child announces with a sense of finality, "Mommy, I don't ever want to get married. I just want to live forever with you and daddy." While our heads know that eventually they will think differently, our hearts want to believe them. And as a result we sometimes forget that parenting is a temporary job.

I recently spent some time with the very distinguished author, lecturer, and counselor, Dr. Lofton Hudson. On consecutive nights he spoke on the subject of marriage to several different age groups. In all of them he had a question-and-answer session. The issue of "releasing our children" kept coming up. His advice made lots of sense. He insisted that we learn to turn loose of our children by reminding ourselves from the beginning that our job is only temporary. We are equipping them for life so that when they leave we will be ready for the separation.

One very important caution for this period is to emphasize the continued development of the husband-wife relationship. This is a needed warning because the period of parenthood parallels the development of career. The foundations for later problems have often been laid in a family where a woman has given herself totally to the rearing of children and the man has given himself totally to the advancement of his career. In the process they have given little to each other.

But if parenthood is seen as a challenge that has within it the potential for great growth, development, and enrichment, then when the children are all gone you will have two people with a stronger marriage and better equipped to face the next phase of their lives.

Empty Nest/Retirement

There is something very traumatic about having your last child leave home. Perhaps your last one is attending university but he/she is gone and you know it. And that awareness writes "finis" to a most significant period of life called parenthood. Parents continue to love their grown children and remain interested in their lives—

but never again will there be that close parent-child relationship that existed in the family home.

For many couples this freedom offers one of the best times in life. Since they have prepared for it, instead of grieving they are able to enjoy the liberty to do all the things impossible before because of responsibility for children. I see many couples like this and they are a joy to watch. Usually they are people who have been working on their relationship all along. Their friendships are supportive and their activities have meaning for their lives. They are busy people who are unselfish in their relationship with one another.

Frank and Jeannette's youngest has been gone four years and they are having the time of their lives. For one thing, they didn't wait until the last minute to begin planning for the "empty nest." Through the years each developed outside interests. Jeannette loved music and involved herself with the choir. Frank taught a Sunday school class. They joined together to make their home a gathering place for young couples from the class. Both had a wealth of outside friends. But more than anything else they were aware that this phase of their lives was going to be different.

Their son was a senior in high school when I mentioned to Frank that it seemed to me he and Jeannette were doing more and more things together. "Yes," he said with a big grin on his face. "You see, next year it's back to just the two of us. I don't want to look across the table and say, 'My name is Frank. I fish a lot. What do you do?'" Folks like that make the empty nest fun.

But for some the period immediately after the children leave is one of the most difficult times of life. This is especially true of mothers who have devoted themselves almost exclusively to "mothering" their children. Suddenly the children are gone and mother doesn't know what to do with herself. She can become depressed, bored, or even physically ill. A terrible sense of uselessness can descend on her at this time. What she's good at doesn't need doing any more.

So mother looks to her husband for sympathy and discovers that he is at the very peak of his career and is finding a great deal of fulfillment in what he is doing. Since he has not made the emotional investment in parenting which his wife has, he does not have as much sympathy for what is happening to her and her needs. This can become a really explosive situation if help is not found.

When retirement comes the roles are almost completely reversed. The wife continues doing what she had been doing with some fulfillment. This time it is the husband who is at loose ends. But with retirement come the complications of less money and failing health. All of these add pressures to the marriage relationship. There is that need to be as independent as possible, as long as possible, in as many areas as possible.

Some of the best marriages I've found have been among couples in retirement. Nothing is more encouraging to some of us who are younger than to see people in retirement moving out with a sense of excitement into new areas of involvement and activity. Kenneth and Nelda are most representative of a host of the couples I know. We first met when I was speaking in their city and they were my hosts for lunch. Nelda was a professor at the University of Houston and Kenneth was a railroad man. Even then they were people with an interest in others. (I've decided that there's just no way people who think only of themselves can ever be happy.)

Since moving to Houston I've watched both of them

go through the process of retirement. Kenneth was first. He had a year when Nelda was still working. That was the year the Vietnamese refugees came and he assumed a major responsibility for several families. After Nelda retired they took the usual big trip. But now they've settled down to living in retirement. That period which is so depressing to many for them is a time for new blossoms. People who, like Kenneth and Nelda, begin early to build relationships, involving themselves in interests outside themselves, come to retirement with choices and opportunities for further growth.

The family never ceases to change: There is a dynamic about it. Whether it is a bride and groom learning to share their lives together, parents busy preparing children for life, or a couple enjoying once again being alone together, there are challenges and opportunities all along the way. Those families which work on dealing with the normal and natural crises as they arise will be strengthened by the process. And they will find it much easier to deal with the destructive pressures of the society in which they must function.

Social Pressures

In addition to the normal internal problems that are a part of being a family there are many pressures exerted upon the family from outside, from society. Some of these pressures have their source in the changes brought about in our lives by urbanization. Some grow out of social revolutions which are taking place. This is especially true as it relates to how women view themselves. A certain amount of pressure comes from the advocacy of alternative life styles being suggested as substitutes for marriage and the family. In all of this the media is involved both as a reflector of the values of the people and a creator of attitudes. These pressures need to be understood and their potential for good or bad upon the family evaluated. When we see what these pressures are, then we need to deal with them.

Few aspects of modern life put more pressure on a family than a man's career. A man's sense of identity is tied up with his job. If the average man is asked, "Who are you?" he will not give his name but will tell what he does. He will say, "I work for Exxon," or "I'm a lawyer," or "I sell pharmaceuticals."

Society usually defines success in terms of accomplishment within a career with little reference to the private life of the person and often no reference to his family. Society forgets that people are a part of a system which includes a family. A corporation will often move a man with little awareness of what that move may be doing to his wife and children. It is possible for a man's career to become the number one competitor for his family.

Years ago the wife of a friend of mine began to have some deep emotional problems which she was unable to handle. The husband sent his wife to a very reliable psychiatrist. After he had spent considerable time with the woman he reported to her husband, "Your wife feels that she has to compete with your job for affection and attention. If her competition were another woman she would probably know how to cope with that. But she does not know how to deal with your career as her competition." This is a pressure which continues to arise in modern urban life.

The Two-Career Family

Another growing pressure on the family is the two-career situation. On the night Barbara and I had our first date, as I sat in the parlor of the dormitory waiting for her I began reading a new book I had just discovered. It was Pauline and Elton Trueblood's book, *The Recovery of Family Life.* Even then the potential problems for the family of the two-career household were being discussed.

While I'm convinced that the two-career family is here to stay, I'm equally sure that it will create certain pressures upon the relationship. For years the only jobs available to women were extremely low-paying. While the small amount the wife earned was a help with the family budget, her job was no threat to her husband's ego. Now more and more women are being given jobs commensurate with their education and ability. While tensions over shared housework have been around for a long time we will soon be dealing with some new ones. In a two-career family the couple has to come to grips with the amount of time and energy devoted by both partners to jobs outside the home. This is a relatively new pressure which has to be faced wisely and openly.

At the same time the second career is gaining momentum in our society, those women who decide to stay home and devote themselves exclusively to homemaking are being lampooned. A recent writer asked what would happen to dentistry if suddenly all the articles in the papers, all the interviews on radio or television, or all the humorists began to make fun of it. The answer was obvious. That vocation which is ridiculed loses its attractiveness for those seeking a place to invest their lives. This is what is happening to the vocation of homemaking. The pressure is so strong that individuals who choose to go that direction are feeling the need to "defend" their decision.

On my desk is a long handwritten letter from a mother of two small children. Her letter is almost a classic statement of the rationale behind her decision to "choose to stay home rather than plunge into the exciting worlds of business or education." Hers is such a healthy approach. She has made her decisions in the light of well-thought-out goals which relate to her marriage and family. Not everyone who feels this pressure will be so wise.

An Unfriendly World

The society in which we live is not always friendly to the family. The world into which I was born and in which I spent my younger years fostered a good feeling about the family. And in my community the school, the churches, and all the other institutions of society were highly supportive of the idea of marriage and the family. This is not true of the world in which my children are growing up.

Some years ago I had a programming position with my denomination. I was based in Atlanta, Georgia. Since I was responsible for the entire denomination I did a great deal of traveling. One day as I boarded one of the big Delta jets I noticed that the stewardess checking our boarding passes had a large engagement ring. When after take-off she came by to serve soft drinks I commented on how attractive the ring was and asked when she was getting married.

She quickly told me the day, hour, month, place— and gave me a thumbnail sketch of the young man who was to be her husband.

I thanked her and said, "I wish you well in your marriage." Then I told her briefly how happy Barbara and I had been in our marriage and that our relationship was better after several years of marriage than when we had first married.

After she finished serving everyone she came and sat beside me, talking about her feelings on the subject of marriage. The thing I remember most vividly about our conversation was her comment: "I've been wearing this ring for over three months and you are my first passenger to say a kind word about marriage."

I tried to excuse the others to whom she had talked by suggesting that they had probably been tired or were probably just kidding. But she would not accept that explanation.

"No," she said, "I'm convinced that there is developing in this country a deep cynicism about marriage—and it frightens me."

That young stewardess's words have been almost prophetic because now in our society the idea of getting married at all is being seriously questioned.

Glen Campbell is one of the rather wholesome entertainers on the American music scene. Did you ever notice the lyrics of his hit song, "Gentle on My Mind"? It speaks of leaving a bedroll behind the sofa and coming and going at will. It extolls not being tied together by words written on a document. That document was a marriage license and the words were the vows. His song is a classic statement of the idea that the best relationships are the casual ones, those that allow us to come and go, which do not tie us down. The song idealizes a relationship that does not have the deep, abiding commitment which must characterize true marriage.

A Look at the Media

No influence is greater in gathering up all the pressures of society and pressing them upon the family than the media. There was a time when many people considered the media to be amoral. It could be used for either good or bad. Now the feeling that the media is essentially immoral is developing. One of the sharpest critics of the media today is Malcolm Muggeridge, who himself has been involved successfully in every phase of media in Great Britain for more than fifty years. Recently he gave a series of lectures which were published in a book entitled *Christ and the Media* (Eerdmans, 1978). The essence of his attack upon the media is that it inverts reality. He says that the media, whether doing the news, a documentary, or a comedy series, tends to make fantasy seem real and reality seem fictional.

While I have certain reservations about some of the positions Muggeridge takes, my own observation of the media is that as a whole it is not good for the family. The media pleads innocence when someone challenges what they are broadcasting, claiming they are simply reflecting society. But there is a sense in which they are also creating values (or the lack of values).

Recently I began carrying on correspondence with a certain television network. In one of their shows they had suggested that having sexual intercourse was a normal and healthy part of sex education for a sixteen-year-old boy. The condescending manner in which my questions were answered made it clear to me that people who are trying to build moral and spiritual values into their children need to begin raising serious questions about morals in the media.

The more serious questions which need to be raised have to do with all the creative things left undone while we watch reruns of old situation comedies. There are two television sets at our house. One is a big old cabinet model which we bought about ten years ago when I was going to be on nationwide TV. The family wanted to see it all "in color." The other is a smaller transistorized set up in the back bedroom. Several weeks ago both broke at the same time. At first we had the usual withdrawal pains. We didn't know how to tell time or what to do with ourselves. Then after a day or two we didn't even miss them. It was nice. We didn't miss a thing. The little set is fixed now, but at our house we are rethinking the role the media is going to play for us.

If a person wanted to he could concentrate so much on the problems of life that he would be overwhelmed. But that isn't necessary. Problems are built into life and having them is a sign we aren't dead. We are problem solvers. And in the process of working out problems we grow and develop.

Society surrounds the family with all sorts of pressures. This is because the family is a social institution. We influence society and it influences us. But the real good news is that even in a world with the rapid and radical changes ours is experiencing, the family is able to adapt and function and do its work.

The whole key to how the family deals with its challenges has to do with the marital pair. How the husband and wife understand marriage and their roles in it determine what they will do. How we function as parents, as fathers, as mothers, and how our children see the family depends upon this basic couple. The next chapter deals with the nature and goals of this relationship.

For further thinking and discussion:

1. Do you consider the media a plus or minus in accomplishing the goals of your family?
2. What changes have taken place in your family during the past two years which call for adjustments?
3. When you first married what did you discover about each other that was a surprise?
4. What do you and your mate intend to do when the children are gone?
5. What stage of parenting do you think was most difficult for your parents to deal with?

3

The Marital Pair

Seeing a good family in operation encourages me. It's exciting to sit on the sidelines and watch such a family function. I watch them meet each other's needs, communicating with each other at many different levels, making decisions, and solving problems—and I marvel. Each member of the family has his own uniqueness, but he also shows a love and appreciation for the others. It's even profitable to watch a good family handle the inevitable conflicts. Such families can share themselves with others without any sense of loss to themselves. Everyone knows families like this.

As a single young man around an active, healthy family, I recall feeling a little bit of envy and asking a lot of questions. In my heart I knew that one day I wanted a family like that. The questions all came as I wondered how these families came to be that way. Were they just lucky to be so happy or did they *do* something? Could anyone who really wanted it have a family like that—or was it reserved for just a few high achievers? What was the key?

It took me a long time but I found the answers to most of those questions I asked so long ago. I discovered that chance has nothing to do with an excellent family—it takes work! While there is a lot of work involved in building a good family, the goal is within the reach of most of us. But the best thing I've learned is the identity of the most important ingredient in a good family.

The foundation for everything which happens in the family, for good or for bad, is laid by the kind of relationship which the husband and wife develop in their marriage.

The family begins when a man and woman join their lives together in marriage. Everything is at stake in the relationship of that basic pair. If it is a good relationship then that marriage is like a house "built upon a rock" and all the winds and rains of life can beat upon it and it will stand and function and meet the needs of those in it.

There is no way to build a happy, effective family on an inadequate relationship between a husband and wife. It is like building a house "upon the sand" and the pressures and problems which would be handled easily by other families will cause this one to shake and possibly even crumble.

Preparation for Relationship

People who want good marriage relationships need to make good preparation. I have the feeling that the younger generation is a bit more aware of the dynamics of relationships. This awareness is reflecting itself in their increased interest in getting ready for marriage. Several years ago I began to be convinced that by the time a young couple sits down with the minister to plan their wedding there are a few practical helps which can be given but little substantive counseling. To see if there might be an interest among young people in thinking a little bit about marriage before they find themselves planning their wedding, I prepared a talk which I gave on a number of university campuses around the country. I called it "Don't Ruin Your Marriage While You Are Still Single." In the talk I dealt with what is happening to the idea of marriage today, what marriage is all about, and how the ways they were thinking now could be either helpful or harmful to their future marriage. The response was good and told me what I needed to know. People are concerned about the institution of marriage and are wondering if there's something they can do to prepare for it.

Dick Stafford, our minister to single adults, felt that since our church had virtually pioneered in designing ministries to the formerly married we ought to put together and promote a seminar on "Getting Ready for Marriage." In the announcements and promotion it was emphasized that this was not a premarital counseling course for those who were engaged but was open to any single who wanted to make an investment in a future marriage. We even encouraged high school seniors to come. It was interesting that those we counseled with told us that "this had been tried before" and that we shouldn't be surprised if no one came. We had a full house from the first session and have run the series several times with equal success. From the response we received, it is evident that there are more and more people who know the importance of a good marriage and are willing to do some thinking about it.

The first step in preparation for a good marriage is to give that relationship priority in your life. When people are talking about their future they often speak about their vocational goals. They make plans in the light of these goals. No one seems embarrassed either to ask or answer questions about what "do you plan to do." Marriage is much more of a private affair than the jobs at which we work but it is still of importance to fix in our minds and hearts goals which we would like to accomplish. This might not be a decision you would announce from the rooftop. But it is something you ought to talk about to those people who know and love you, and are interested in your dreams and goals in life.

People also need to begin thinking both about what they would like in a mate and what they would like to bring to the relationship. Many people do *some* thinking about the basis of the attraction. If two people are considering a lifetime together I would naturally assume they are physically attracted to each other. I do not feel that a marriage relationship can be totally platonic. For two people to be physically attracted to each other is a wonderful thing. But that fact alone gives no assurance of a good marriage relationship. A normal, healthy adult could be physically attracted to any number of people.

A second thing to consider would be: do you know each other well and respect each other as persons? So much of the healthiness of a relationship has to do with our acceptance of each other as persons and mutual trust. People who are strangers to each other in a courtship are apt to be enemies in a marriage. This is why hasty marriages are so risky. Taking time to be with each other and with others under all kinds of circumstances is vital in building relationships.

I met Barbara while we were in graduate school together. Although we had fallen in love and were engaged, I had not met her parents. Meeting the people she worked with in Nashville had helped me get to know her better. But about a month before our wedding I went with her to south Georgia to meet her family and her relatives and the friends from church and community. I really loved her before I made the trip but words cannot express the sense in which my feelings about her were confirmed as I came to know her through the eyes of her family and friends.

A third question to ask yourself is: do we really have common values and goals for our lives? Hardly a month goes by but that I am called to sit down with a young couple in trouble because they have conflicting values and goals. In the process of the conversation it becomes apparent to both of them that they are looking for different things from life and that these differences are not superficial but are deeply rooted. On occasions I have asked, "Tell me, with such diametrically opposed views of life, why did you get married in the first place?" The answer is always the same: "We just loved each other so much and we didn't realize how the other felt until after we were married."

Most of us assume that the person whom we plan to marry wants the same things from the marriage that we do—and has the same ideas about marriage that we have. This probably comes from the crazy notion that people in love read each other's minds. They don't. The number of situations where the marriage relationship was strained by husbands and wives having strong feelings about something but failing to communicate those feelings are legion. The man assumed that after the wedding his wife would quit work. She planned that after the honeymoon she would resume her career. But neither brought it up until after the wedding. The man who never wanted children and the woman who assumed they would have children suddenly found themselves married!

A fourth thing you should consider is the person's religious commitment. You will note that I said "commitment" and not membership. Just as there is a religious dimension to man and to life, there is a profoundly religious dimension to marriage. I think that two people who take God seriously have more going for them in their marriage. If one person has a vital faith and the other only a nominal relationship to some church it can be a source of tension in the marriage, especially when the time comes to act out in front of your children your moral and spiritual values. When I plan to marry someone, I ought to accept that person the way he/she is. If that person's life is a big problem to me, I ought not marry. Never marry someone with plans to change him/her. It would be better to find someone whose commitment already matches yours.

What Do We Promise?

It was to be a quiet wedding in my study. Ten minutes before the agreed-upon time I heard a knock on the outer door of my office. When I opened it there stood my friend, Jim, all smiles, with the marriage license in one hand and his bride-to-be's hand in the other. Before I could usher the two of them into the study he announced, "I'm ready, pastor, now what do I have to promise?"

His question is one everyone who wants a good marriage ought to ask long before he even thinks about getting married. Nothing is better preparation for marriage than getting a good understanding of the nature of the relationship. There *are* promises to make and to keep. The next time you are at a wedding listen carefully to the vows. If they are in the beautiful English of the King James era, paraphrase them in your mind. These vows have their roots in the biblical and historical ideals for the marriage relationship. They give a clear picture of what the marital bond is.

There has been a lot of innovation in wedding ceremonies during the past decade. This has been especially true of the music which has been used. Some of the changes have been nothing more than substituting this decade's sentimental song for the last decade's sentimental song. There's really no difference in the "I'll Be Loving You Always" which was sung at weddings during the fifties and the "We've Only Just Begun" of today.

One of the most interesting innovations has been the desire of a number of couples to write their own vows and memorize them for the ceremony. Though it always makes me a little nervous, wondering if they'll remember their vows, I like the idea of the individuals giving some serious thought to what they are promising each other. The only request I ever make of them is that however contemporary or personal the words may be, they reflect the kind of commitment to each other which is at the heart of the marriage relationship.

While our first child was a preschooler and our second was on the way Barbara had a period when she had to spend most of her time in bed. I was finishing my doctoral work, teaching a full load as a graduate assistant, and doing some outside speaking. To add to it all Nancy came down with chicken pox. To relieve the itching several times a day she had to be given a "starch" bath. Though many thoughtful neighbors and friends brought dishes of food by from time to time, the main responsibility for wife, daughter, house, and classes fell to me.

As the week wore on I wore out, physically and emotionally. It seemed that before I finished one responsibility another was starting. One night Barbara and Nancy were both asleep and I was standing over a sink full of dishes feeling sorry for myself. I suddenly remembered one of the episodes in the cartoon life of Blondie and Dagwood in which he finds himself involved in a lot of things he hadn't anticipated when he married. He said, "They should have put this in the ceremony." Those were my sentiments exactly. Then it dawned upon me. It *was* in the ceremony. I could even remember saying it. It went like this. "In sickness and in health, for better or for worse." I had a little laugh *with* myself and *at* myself and discovered a little healthier appreciation for the promises I had made.

Forsaking All Others

In describing the relationship between Adam and Eve, the first book of the Bible states, "That is why a man leaves his father and mother and is united to his wife, and the two become one flesh" (Gen. 2:24). This is the passage Jesus quoted in his discussion of marriage in the gospels. Hovering in the background of this passage is the idea that marriage had its origin with God and that our maleness and femaleness have their beginning with God. But in addition there are three basic ideas which have to do with the nature of the marriage relationship.

First is the idea that marriage is an *exclusive* relationship. This is what the "forsaking all others" means in the ceremony. There is more here than meets the eye. Does this mean that when we get married all ties with the family in which a person was reared must be severed? No, but it does mean that the decision to get married will place you in a different kind of relationship, a relationship in which the commitment to the new family created by the marriage takes precedence over the relationship with parents. This can be extremely painful for children who haven't left home emotionally and are still very dependent upon parents. It can also be painful for parents who do not know how to turn loose of their children. But when the break is made and the parental relationship is reestablished on more mature bases there are rich rewards for all involved.

Does the exclusiveness of this relationship mean that both partners give up all the friends they had before they were married? No, but it is clearly established that the husband-wife relationship is to have priority over all others. It would probably be a mistake for a couple to get married and withdraw from all their previous friends. Many needs that individuals have can be met in meaningful friendships with both men and women. These should be encouraged and clear boundaries set for them.

One of the real problems which our secular society has is this: it does not understand that for a marriage to work and a relationship to be healthy it has to be monogamous sexually. Husbands and wives make a commitment of sexual faithfulness to each other. From any perspective no good case can be made for sexual promiscuity. People who want to build a good husband-wife relationship should begin by planning to be faithful to one another.

Woven into the very fabric of the idea of marriage is the idea of commitment. This means that to really understand marriage you have to go against the current of today's thinking, which is nervous about deep and long-term commitments. There is an almost crazed crying out to be "free" and independent and unstructured. It is my contention that these so-called "apostles of personal freedom" are really prisoners of their own desires and frightened to death of true love which is willing to make a commitment. Immaturity and self-centeredness make us afraid of commitments. People who make commitments are the freest people I know.

Sharing the Whole Life

The second basic ideal for marriage is that it is to be an *extensive* relationship. The term "exclusive" builds a fence around the relationship and defines its priority status. The term "one flesh" defines the extensive relationship inside that fence. It is to be the sharing of whole lives with each other.

The most obvious meaning of "one flesh" refers to the bodies joined in sexual union. When I was in an ethics class in school marriage was defined as taking place when a man and woman came together as husband and wife and consummated the marriage in sexual intercourse. To this day most states will grant an annulment on the basis that the marriage was never consummated physically.

But there is a much larger significance to the idea of "one flesh." Marriage is so much more than society sanctioning the sexual activity of two people. The broader concept sees "one flesh" as having to do with the husband and wife sharing all of their lives together. There is the sharing of thoughts and feelings, dreams and aspirations, problems and triumphs. The modern notion that sex is what gives meaning to the rest of the relationship has it backward. It is the sharing of the experiences of life together as husband and wife which makes sex more meaningful.

The idea of "one flesh" in no way diminishes the individuals and their need for development. The need to make this clear was dramatized for me at a wedding several years ago. I had never seen what is called a "unity candle" in a ceremony. What I saw shook me. By the altar there were three candles. The two outside ones, representing the bride and groom, were lighted. The center one, representing the new relationship of marriage, was unlighted. After the minister pronounced the couple husband and wife they turned to the trio of candles and each took an outside candle and together lighted the larger candle. Up to that point, the symbolism was simple and moving.

Then something happened I was not really prepared for. Each took his/her lighted candle and blew it out. I wanted to shout, "No." In a sense each was saying now that this new relationship was formed they no longer existed as individuals, it seemed to me. That's not so. All three exist, the bride, the groom, and the marriage.

Today, when a couple asks me to perform their wedding and want to use the unity candle, I agree on one condition. I ask them to please not blow out their candle and to please continue to grow and develop as individuals because the middle candle, the marriage, depends on it.

A Permanent Commitment

The phrase in the ceremony "till death do us part" speaks eloquently to the whole idea that marriage is a commitment to a *permanent* relationship. This is a part of the desire of everyone who goes into a marriage and is God's plan for this part of our lives. The ideal is put there because he loves us and knows that we will be happier if we enter into a permanent relationship.

I'm constantly reading books and articles in which authors are dealing in a condescending manner with the whole idea of a man and woman joining their lives together forever. They marshall all sorts of hollow-sounding arguments in favor of what they call "tandem" relationships. I'm of the opinion that much of this sort of writing is a confession that these people are not capable of handling a permanent relationship. It is an effort to justify their own life style with some pseudo-scholarly writing.

During the last five years I have worked closely with more than 2200 formerly married men and women. In the process of helping them begin their lives again I have never had a single one of them suggest to me that the ideal ought to be changed. On the contrary, each of them still feels that marriages ought to be permanent.

The wisdom of God's admonition is obvious. Permanence provides an atmosphere of security for the partners. It allows them to live day-by-day using their energy to enrich the relationship. This aura of permanence makes it easier to deal with problems instead of running. It is better for the children *and* for the parents. This is why those who plan to marry should not come to the relationship with any reservation. Permanence is the nature of the commitment.

Nurturing the Relationship

The reception has been over long enough that you've emptied all the rice out of everything. The wedding gifts have been unwrapped and the "thank you" notes have been written. The relatives have all been informed that you made it safely back from the honeymoon. The phones are off vacation. You're both back at work. The newness of your marriage is still showing but you're beginning to feel comfortable with each other and it's a good feeling. Now, what do you do?

Number one, begin nurturing your marriage relationship.

Number two, begin nurturing your marriage relationship.

Number three, begin nurturing your marriage relationship.

If there were a four through ten it would be the same. This relationship is not just the sum of the two of you but something more which you have formed by joining your lives together. This relationship has a uniqueness just as a person does.

I would not diminish the other tasks which need to be performed in a marriage. It is true that the individual self has to be nurtured. This is needed by both husband and wife as individuals. It is also true that when children come they must be nurtured. And the nurture of the self, the marriage, and the children must be kept in balance. It would be difficult, however, to overemphasize the importance of nurturing the marriage relationship.

Over the past thirty years I have suffered alongside numerous couples whose marriages ended in divorce. In almost every instance the marriage failed because somewhere in the process that vital husband-wife relationship was neglected. Often the couple kept busy with work and children and even church while the relationship died. When the storms came they had no stamina with which to weather the problem.

Two of the most important skills which will help

you to develop your marriage are communicating skills and decision-making skills. You need to learn how to talk to each other and listen to each other because that's the only way you are going to find out constructively what's going on in each other's mind. Since you love each other and really want to make each other happy, what better thing could you do with each other than communicate what pleases you or what makes you unhappy? If you can trust each other enough to share your feelings it will keep anger from building up. The couple who really work at communicating with one another at every level about every subject are creating excellent tools with which to strengthen their relationship.

Learning to make decisions is important because newly married people have many decisions to make and will continue to have them all their lives. Nothing can make things run more smoothly than learning how to make decisions small and large. It may be a little awkward at first, since having to involve another person is new. There may be tensions at first because each is apt to assume the process will be like it was in the homes in which they were reared (forgetting that there were two distinct home environments involved). There could even be conflict since mixed into some of the decisions will be other agendas like priorities and goals. But only a couple who can communicate and make decisions together can go into the business of making their marriage stronger.

What is it that nurtures a relationship, that feeds it, that makes it stronger? The list could be endless and you can add to it. (1) The things you do together as a couple. (2) The problems you work on together. (3) Being with other friends together. (4) Deciding who your friends will be and the activities you will be involved in together. (5) Discovering how much privacy each of you needs and learning to honor it. (6) Involving yourselves in some ministry to others together.

It doesn't sound all that profound, does it? All we are talking about is two people who love each other and are married to each other developing skills in meeting each other's needs and having their own needs met. It may sound simple but the implications for you in terms of happiness and fulfillment are profound.

Love, Love, Love

There is a great deal of discussion today about the roles of husband and wife in the home and the basis of their relationship with each other. Because entire books are written on this one subject I would not pretend in this brief space to deal exhaustively with the subject.

Self-giving love is to be the basis of the relationship between the husband and wife. Of this I am convinced. I believe that the intent of the Word of God has been overlooked by some who have misunderstood the meaning of the scripture: "Wives, be subject to your husbands as to the Lord" (Eph. 5:22). To give an orientation to this passage I want to guide us in a brief look at its context and application to the marriage relationship.

First, whatever "be subject" means it applies to both husbands and wives because the previous verse says, "Be subject *to one another* out of reverence for Christ" (Eph. 5:21, italics mine).

Second, the verb form which Paul used when applying this word to Christ, church members, or wives means a voluntary attitude of giving in, cooperating, and assuming responsibility. It speaks of a kind of total humility, gentleness, and mutual love. Nowhere in its use is there the idea of blind obedience or of legislative or judicial power.

Here are two examples: Christ made himself "subject" to the father without losing his dignity. The Roman senator yielded to another without becoming an underling.

Third, the whole discussion is in the context of a husband who exhibits Christlike love. There is not the slightest hint of male superiority or female inferiority here. We need to remember that this is a husband-wife discussion and not a male-female one. Also remember that they were both members of Christ's body in whom it was said that "There is no such thing as Jew and Greek, slave and freeman, male and female; for you are all one person in Christ Jesus" (Gal. 3:28).

Fourth, the husband is to give leadership. His leadership is interpreted, qualified, and limited by the example of Christ's love for the church. If Christ's relationship with the church is the model then the husband should enable the wife to grow, should spend time with her, should nourish her, and should put her needs first whatever the cost to himself. This leadership spells itself out as loving care. He is *leader* and not *boss*.

Fifth, love for one another is to be the dominant theme for the relationship. I'm convinced that the issue is never who's in charge but the basis of the relationship. People who have an unselfish love for one another can work things out. People who really love each other can make mistakes and start over with one another. People who love each other can survive without always getting their own way. People who love each other can adapt themselves to one another.

This kind of love at work in the daily experience of a husband and wife can bring an added dimension to all their relationships.

Look around you at what you consider one of the best families you know in terms of functioning and meeting the needs of all its members. Remove all the kids and in-laws and grandparents and what you will probably find at the heart of it will be a husband and wife with a solid relationship. If they'll talk to you about it you will probably discover they have made a vocation of nurturing that relationship and have found the rewards worth it. The best preparation for parenting is a strong, growing relationship between husband and wife.

For further thinking and discussion:

> 1. Why is "love at first sight" a risky foundation for marriage?
> 2. When should two people planning to marry begin developing good communication skills?
> 3. What activities and experiences you have had together have contributed most to the strengthening of your marriage?
> 4. What is the most important single ingredient in a husband-wife relationship?
> 5. How are major decisions which involve everyone made in your family?

4

Encouragement for Parents

The person who said "husbands and wives are not the same as fathers and mothers" should be given a prize for understatement. I watched this communicated with good-natured humor one night with several young couples. Of those present, Dave and Jana were the only couple who did not have children and their first was due almost any day.

The other husbands in the group decided to prepare Dave for parenthood by explaining some of the "changes" which were about to come into his life. They discussed the changes which would come in his eating habits, his sleep routine, and his relationships with his in-laws. They went on to describe how the beautiful pin-striped suit he was wearing would look with burp marks on the lapel. It was all that kind of light-hearted kidding people do when anticipating an event everyone is excited about. As I listened with a great deal of pleasure I realized that there is really nothing which can adequately prepare a couple for the joy of parenthood nor the challenge and excitement of parenting.

I'm in a very awkward place from which to write this chapter. When I was twenty-five, I had been a pastor for several years. Each year during Christian Home Week I addressed myself to the subject of the family and had some very pointed things to tell the parents about the rearing of their children. All this before I experienced parenthood myself. If I had waited four years to write this book then all my children would have "left the nest." Then I could look back over my years of parenting with a degree of "creative forgetfulness" and tell you with a certain self-righteous air "how I succeeded as a parent." But the truth is that I am in the very middle of parenting.

There is no place apart where I can stand and see more clearly than the rest of you. As a parent, I have the same aspirations you have for your children. The same pressures you feel from the world in which you live are upon me. And often I feel the same sense of inadequacy all parents experience at times. The advice I give you is applied to myself and of the encouragement that I pass on to you I will keep some for myself.

No activity in which couples participate requires a larger investment or brings a larger return than parenting. The parent-child relationship has more potential for fulfillment than any relationship I know. While newspaper and broadcast journalists busy themselves with interviews of people involved in both interesting and exotic vocations, bringing "quality" to parenting is the most important task confronting our society today. And one of the nice things about parenting is that it can be learned. Parenting is not some intuitive skill which you either have or don't have. Babies are born but parenting skills are developed.

As parents, you are the most important influence in your children's lives. You have them first, and they

67

are yours for the longest period of time. Parenting involves the most vital human relationship. Sometimes children have to be reared outside the family situation because of circumstances. But this is always done with an awareness that there is no adequate substitute for parents who love and care and take parenting seriously.

Whether you live in an apartment or a condominium, a duplex or a house on a lot with shrubs and flowers—whether it is an expensive home you own or a run-down place you are renting—it is not the "house" but the "home," the family, which makes the difference. The home creates the environment for the development of persons.

Single Parenting

Parenting responsibility is essentially the same whether a couple or just one parent is involved. An increasing number of families have but one parent in the home. This situation presents a difficult but not impossible task. Many single-parent families are doing well. Without exception, the ones I am aware of are making up for the absent mate by plugging into a network of support groups which become allies of the parent and the children. A father or mother with sole responsibility for children will find immeasurable help from Sunday school teachers, scouting, choirs, camps, grandparents, and close adult friends. The basic needs of children and the goals of parenting are the same whether done alone or with help from a mate.

Creating Conditions for Growth

Though I have lived most of my adult life in the city I have continued to be fascinated by farming. It probably goes back to watching my mother and father manage their rather large garden. Even after we moved to the city they would rent a couple of vacant lots and "make" a garden.

Usually they would get some farmer to do the initial plowing of the garden. Dad called it "turning the ground." Then with hoes and rakes and a lot of back-bending work they would begin to prepare the soil for planting. There were always clods to break up and small rocks to remove. During this part of the operation I usually followed along behind the plow filling a tin can with the fish worms which had been uncovered.

My parents were aware of the varying ways the beds and rows were prepared for different vegetables. They had a knowledge of what seeds could stand cold and could be planted early and what had to be held back until there wasn't a chance of frost. They knew how to protect the plants from disease and insects.

While they couldn't create plants or seeds or make them grow, they could create the conditions in which that growing would take place. And we enjoyed the produce of their knowledge by having fresh vegetables on the table all summer and home-canned vegetables in the winter.

In many ways those of us who are parents are like good gardeners, except our crop is more important. We cannot create life and we cannot control growth. But we can create the conditions in which it is most apt to take place. Parenting may make necessary the plowing up of old routines and the removal of those elements in a relationship which won't provide a good atmosphere for growth. It will involve learning more about children: their needs, wants, and growth patterns. It should involve being sensitive to all the "insects and diseases" which could keep them from blossoming and having a fruitful life. Such involvement will take time and patience because both gardening and parenting are processes.

There needs to be awareness of the timing in meeting needs. We must be aware of a sense of partnership between us and God. The gardener needs the "you send the sunshine and I'll hoe the weeds" kind of feeling about what he does. Parents, too, feel the importance of what they do in parenting, but they look to God for the part he can play in the process. What greater joy could come to parents than to see the fruit of their labor in a happy, whole, effective adult who is the product of their home?

Any analogy, like a parable, is intended to convey one simple truth. You have probably figured out, if you have been trying to think about parenting in terms of gardening, that while the basic thesis is true when you press it too far it breaks down. While we do create the climate for growth, there is a drastic difference between a live baby and radish seeds. Feeding the physical, social, emotional, and spiritual needs of a teenager is vastly more complex than buying a bag of "6–10–6" fertilizer for the garden. Children do not come with instructions attached and the reassuring words that they will "bear fruit seventy-two days from planting."

You are right. Parenting children is very complex and has a dynamic quality which will require all the love, patience, ingenuity, and stamina you have—and sometimes you'll still feel inadequate. The reactions of children are not as predictable as plants. I recall the first emotions of holding our baby daughter in my arms and thinking, *You're a delightful little ball of putty whom God has given us to form into what you need to become.* It wasn't long, however, before I discovered that our little "ball of putty" had a will of her own, a schedule of her own, and was fast developing tastes of her own. Soon she was learning to put her hands on her hips, shake her head from side to side, look me straight in the eye, and say, "No."

Those parents who have just had a confrontation with a teenage child should identify with one of the stories which Billy Graham enjoys telling as he speaks to young people about their relationships with their parents. A man and his son were in the middle of a heated argument. Finally the son in great anger shouted, "I didn't ask to be born into this family." To which the hurt and angry father replied, "I know. And if you *had* asked, the answer would have been no." Seeds never argue with the gardener—but sons and daughters are so much nicer to have around than carrots and string beans!

Not only are the reactions of children unpredictable, the whole family situation is infinitely more complex than gardening. This is why when you read a book about parenting or hear a lecture or read an article on the subject, you should always beware when it begins, "All you have to do is . . ." You can be assured that the author of these words still views parenting as some fairly simple, fairly static, follow the "ten simple rules" sort of activity. Nothing could be further from the truth.

One of my favorite professors in graduate school told of going to hear a rather noted author lecture on parenting. The auditorium was filled with parents and the man spoke on "The Way to Rear Children." When it came time for discussion, a harried mother of four who was discovering in the laboratory of her own home how complex children really are stood to her feet and in a tone that communicated far more than her words said, "Doctor, I'm the mother of four growing, energetic, active children and I want you to know that there just isn't any *the* way to rear children." Her point was well taken. Nothing lays a better foundation for parenting than the awareness that the task is important, difficult, worth while, and one which parents *can* do if they are willing to pay the price. Children, like adults, are unique—and they must be treated like the individuals they are.

Clarifying Goals

All parents have goals for their children. Sometimes they are fantasy kinds of goals like "growing up to be president" or "being the first woman on the moon." At other times they are unconscious efforts on the part of the parent to meet some unfulfilled need in his own life. Because of this it is not unusual to find a man who never had an opportunity for education pushing his child to "get all you can" or a mother who feels she married too young advising her daughter to "live a little before you settle down." Sometimes the goals are more like a wish or a prayer for your children, a desire in their behalf. Often the goals do not get expressed, talked about by parents, or discussed with children. But always in our minds and hearts we have goals for our children. And one of the best things parents can do for their children is to help them clarify the goals for their lives.

All of our plans for life are dependent upon whether we have a sense of self-worth or self-esteem. This is not the same as conceit. How a person feels about himself is the mainspring that determines success or failure as a human being. A person's self-respect is based upon two convictions. First, "I am lovable." This is another way of saying that I matter and have value because I exist. Second, "I am worth while." This is the affirmation of having something to contribute. These are needs which we bring to childhood and take with us all our lives. They are as necessary to our emotional well-being as oxygen is to our physical survival. Helping our children build a healthy picture of themselves is the key to successful parenthood. Almost everything else we do is built on that.

Home is the best place and parents are the best people for laying the foundation for a healthy image of self. The beginnings take place early in a baby's life. Once, after I had read a penetrating article on the importance of a child's picture of himself I began to wonder what it was my mother and father did to help me accept and like myself. One thing I am sure of is that having little formal schooling neither of them ever used words like "self-esteem" and "self-image." I thought about it for a while and decided I would run it by a friend whose training and experience in this area of family life are considerable.

"Linda," I asked, not knowing whether or not I really wanted to know the answer, "I think I have a fairly healthy view of myself. What do you think my mom and dad did to give that to me?"

She grinned, thought a minute, and replied, "Chafin, it probably started long before the period in your life you can remember. When you were born they began the process of letting you know your worth and value. They fed you, changed your diapers, kept you warm, and took care of all those physical needs. In addition they held you, talked to you, showed you off to relatives and neighbors, and made you a part not only of the family but of the extended family."

She concluded by saying, "Unless you've seen, as I have, a lot of babies who haven't had that, you don't realize how important it is."

73

As children grow older they need to hear expressions of appreciation and encouragement. Compliments are to the inner being what sunshine is to the flower. Children need to be made a part of things, to have responsibilities, to be included in discussions and decisions. All this contributes to their feeling like separate and valuable persons in a family.

This need is acted out every day of our lives. For instance, a man and his wife took their preschool child into a restaurant to eat. When the waitress came to take the order she began with the child. "What would you like, young lady?" The little girl was ready and informed the waitress firmly that she wanted a hamburger, some french fries, and a coke. The mother who had been visiting with her husband turned and argued with her daughter about the order. When the orders finally came, the waitress, to the little girl's delight, had brought her a hamburger, french fries, and a coke. Commenting to her mother about the waitress the preschooler said, "She thinks I'm for real." Those of us who are parents make the largest contribution to our child's sense of self-worth.

There was a period as our children were growing up when if you had asked me what my goals for my children were I probably couldn't have put them into words. If you had mentioned something, I would probably have been able to say, "Yes, I would like that," or "No, never!" as it related to my children's future. I had vague but firm ideas and feelings about what I would hope they would be or do. But I had never organized these ideas in my mind enough to be able to discuss them with my wife or to talk about them to my children. Some of my goals were negative, things I didn't want them to do. Some were just assumptions—they would go to college, for example.

Gradually all these nebulous ideas came together in my thinking so I was able to write them down, talk about them, think about them, evaluate them, and make an effort to "sell" them. You must understand that they are *my* goals for my children and not *their* goals for themselves. I would like for them to consider my goals but whether or not they do so will depend upon them. I once read that in Old Testament times the Hebrew father felt he had three responsibilities to his son: he was to prepare him for the law, fit him for wedlock, and teach him a trade. My goals for our sons *and* daughters are very similar.

First, when they are grown I want them to have a vital faith in God. By this I mean a faith that is their own, which matches in maturity all their other development, and equips them to deal with all the experiences of life and allows them to face death without fear.

Second, I want our children to develop their God-given abilities to their fullest and then to use them for the good of others. This desire is based upon several feelings I have. I'm convinced that the best route to happiness and fulfillment in terms of vocation is to work at something which reflects your skills and which allows growth and development in your greatest area of interest. I'm equally convinced that the law of life is this: all the things you do only for yourself may give a lot of ego-satisfaction but will ultimately be self-destructive. The flip side is that people who use their gifts to enrich the lives of others will find their own lives enriched as a by-product.

Goals Related to Gifts

If this is an overall goal you would entertain for your children, let me make some suggestions. *First,*

75

expose your children to as many experiences as possible. You will learn a great deal about your children's interests and leanings from this. It's interesting to take three children to an exhibit and discover that one is so turned on by models of Da Vinci's inventions he doesn't want to leave—while the others are bored stiff! You will notice that games, toys, books, and television specials are responded to differently by your children in the light of their interests. As you become aware of an interest or special ability encourage it. Help your child to follow up on it. Express an interest in his interest.

Second, resist the temptation to decide for your children what their vocation will be. They need your interest, guidance, encouragement, and support, but ultimately they need from their parents the freedom to decide for themselves and to live with the implications of that decision. I have been surprised how many parents "decide" for their children without any consideration of the child's interest or desire. The parents may love their children but they have made some assumptions about their future which they did not have a right to make.

Several years ago I visited my son's social studies class at the junior high school. I was to give a ten- or fifteen-minute talk on "How People Decide What to Do in Life" and the children were to ask questions. The teacher distributed little index cards and as I talked the boys and girls wrote down what they wanted to ask. It could be about something I had said or something they had always wanted to ask someone on the subject. The questions were varied, direct, and more serious than I expected from sixth graders.

The question which stuck in my mind most was from a little boy who wrote: "My daddy has decided that I will be a dentist. I don't want to be a dentist. Help!" Because of the class schedule we didn't have a chance for private conversation so I wasn't able to discover what his interests or abilities were. I'm well aware that at age twelve many boys don't want to do *anything* dad wants them to do. But I was sure that if the boy's father had known his son's feelings he would have related to him differently.

Third, realize how much help today's children need in separating the truly successful life from the mere making of money. Success has been defined by our society as the ability to make money and translate it into fame, status, or power. Consequently, people have tended to determine the worth of something by how much money you can make doing it. This philosophy has been accompanied by a period of unashamed self-indulgence when it comes to standards of living.

This has done two things. A society which will hardly fund medical research but which makes millionaires out of athletes and rock stars sends a confusing message to young people who really want their gifts and lives to count. The pressure to "have everything" has forced numbers of our most talented young people to move into jobs where they don't have much interest solely because that job paid more. Some of the most miserable people I know are those who know what they're good at and what they enjoy doing but have gone in another direction with their life because they do not want to lower their standard of living. The pressure to adopt purely materialistic goals for our lives is so great that unless we help our children to evaluate current shallow thinking about goals they are apt to be trapped in it.

Help your children understand that not all the meaning in life will come from the job they do for money. So much of the richness in life comes from cultivating and sharing gifts and interest which have no other purpose than the enrichment of life. In my work I associate with many happy and fulfilled people. I do not know a single one who gets all of his fulfillment from his paying job. Human beings have too many interests and abilities just to develop those that are marketable and let the rest shrivel and die.

My *other* goal for our children is for them to have a good marriage. With all that might be said to the contrary taken into consideration, I still feel that there is more potential for happiness and fulfillment within a good marriage than in any other human relationship. I would naturally want that for my children.

From time to time I have discussed these goals with the children, both in a group and as individuals. I've not asked them to promise they will adopt these specific goals for themselves but they are very aware of them. They seem glad that I don't necessarily want them to be rich or famous or powerful. Knowing of my interest and support, they allow me to be a part of the input. They will be making decisions with a set of values we taught them and I'm ready to trust them. They also know that Barbara and I love them and will continue that love whatever direction they go with their lives.

Guiding Through Discipline

Most of us who are parents need a little help in discovering the positive aspects of discipline. I do not know of a single subject which creates more self-doubt among parents. Telling our children "what our fathers would have done to us if we had done what they just did" only tends to underline our sense of frustration. The truth is that we are caught between two extreme positions neither of which is comfortable for us. All of us carry around in our minds the myth of the stern authoritarian father or grandfather who brought order to the family with the leather strap or hickory stick. But somehow when we meet in person that individual who exercises all the power, makes all the rules, and punishes those who break the rules we have absolutely no desire to be like *him.*

Each of us has observed firsthand the totally permissive approach to children. The motives could be legion: a naive notion about the child's needs, a fear of what punishment might do to the personality, a fear of confrontation, or even a lack of interest. But the result is the same. The child is given the power to do whatever he pleases regardless of his or his parents' needs. The results can be disastrous to both the child and the family.

I'm convinced that parents have a better choice than to go with either one of these extremes, since both of them work against the ultimate goal of all discipline—self-discipline. Discipline is the word we use to describe the rules a family lives by and the method employed to make and enforce the rules. A great deal more is involved than "keeping order" in the house.

When children are born they are not able to take care of themselves. They are completely dependent upon their parents to give them guidance in learning how to live. The sole purpose of discipline is to equip this dependent child with ways of living so that when he is on his own and independent he will be able to discipline himself. The most loving thing a parent can do is to prepare his child for self-discipline.

One of the first things we parents need to do is to become sensitive to each child—individualize. While this was true as we discovered their individual gifts and interests, it is also true in matters of discipline. The person who feels that he is being fair by correcting each child in exactly the same way may have forgotten that what is punishment for one child is a stimulus to more disobedience to another. The parent who fits the correction to the nature and disposition of the child has already made a step in the right direction. If the goal is educational and not punitive, as all discipline should be, then the approach which accomplishes the goal with an individual child is best.

Built into the Ten Commandments, which are God's rules for relating to him and to each other, is a statement about how the children are to relate to parents. They are to "obey" and "honor" them. This is so basic that society cannot long function if it is ignored. When children obey, God is honored, parents are encouraged, and the children like themselves better.

To *obey* one's parents implies many things: an eagerness to hear; willingness to heed counsel and to weigh words of advice; readiness to shape our actions under the more mature guidance of parents. This develops in a child self-respect, self-control, and habits of industry.

To *honor* one's parents goes a bit further than obedience. In the whole idea of obedience there is the suggestion of outward conformity. What parent has not had the experience of having a child do *exactly* what he was told but in such a manner that he was really disobeying? (Times like that make memories of the old hickory stick return.) "To honor" means to show the spirit of respect and consideration. It grows out of a genuine love for the parents which is expressed by the way in which they are obeyed.

The New Testament adds an interesting comment

to the discussion of how children are to obey parents. The fathers are warned not to "goad your children to resentment, but give them the instruction, and the correction, which belong to a Christian upbringing" (Eph. 6:4). The suggestion is that discipline ought not to create an angry generation. Discipline ought not to break the spirit, cause self-doubt, or make the child afraid to live.

God disciplines people. It is a part of his love. The thing which keeps his discipline from destroying us is that he separates our worth in his eyes from how he feels about what we have done. Even as he is telling us that he does not like what we have done and is correcting us, he is assuring us of his love for us as persons. Rather than raising questions in their minds about our love for them, our disciplining of our children should be done in such a way that they will eventually see our action as an expression of our love.

Communicating Values

My experience with parents is that most of them are deeply concerned about their children having moral and spiritual values of their own. The thought of their children functioning in a society in which activities and institutions have little or no value system is enough to cause a parent anxiety. While there are times during the process of rearing children when most of us would settle for just "surviving," in our best moments we want our children to be equipped not only physically, emotionally, and socially but also spiritually.

One of the things which must be done is to draw back into the home more responsibility for what our children believe and commit themselves to. In earlier pastoral and agricultural societies it was relatively easy for the home to assume broad functions. The Old Testament reflects this kind of cultural setting. Several generations lived together with the skills being passed from the older to the younger. Social and religious beliefs were built in the family and were woven into the events of working and living.

In the western world that situation has changed. General education has been taken over by the state. Many parents feel that as a result the school is totally responsible and that they are no longer involved. Even worse, most parents do not realize that we are rapidly coming to the place in the public schools where even the suggestion of absolute standards by which right and wrong can be established will no longer be allowed. Our children will soon be taught that everything is relative.

Religious education has been turned over to the church. If you were to evaluate the materials now being used to teach moral and spiritual values to the children by the churches you would be encouraged. Most of these materials combine a faithfulness to the teaching of the scripture with an awareness of how children learn. But we need to remember several things. First, the majority of the children in this country are not enrolled in any structured ongoing moral and spiritual training. Second, those so involved will average attending less than twenty-five times in any one year. Third, if all the children were enrolled and attended each week, those forty-five minutes of study and activity would not be adequate when placed alongside the rest of the week.

With social and recreational life moving out of the family it is easy to see why I'm insisting upon the need for those of us who are parents to do what we can to pull back into the family more of the ultimate responsibilities for our children's learning.

In our kind of society it is impossible to go back to the simple pastoral days with that earlier life style. There is no way in which the family can duplicate what is being done by the school and the church. But there is one thing which we can do as parents, because of the way families function. This cannot be done effectively by either school or church. We can model moral and spiritual values for our children. Modeling is a way of learning from what a person sees and experiences rather than from what is said to him. Behavior does speak louder than words. We have a tendency to copy what we see rather than what we hear. While many of the things going on in our society bother me, I'm convinced that the most effective method I have for counteracting the moral drift in the lives of my children is to match what they hear from me and what they see in me.

One of the finest things a parent can do for a child is to lay a foundation for personal faith and commitment in his life. I hear some parents saying they are not going to try to influence their child in religious matters. I want to believe that what they mean is that they do not want to pressure their child. I would certainly hope that no child would have a parent who did not feel religion was important. A parent must be wise and patient in teaching his children. He must let the child set the pace and take his cues from the child's interest and awareness. Then when a child is ready to make a personal commitment to Christ he needs to be nurtured gently so that the commitment can be related to his life at every stage of his development. The faith of a child is a precious and fragile thing.

Barbara and I were reared in two dissimilar families in different parts of the United States. We were in our twenties before we met. Now we have been married almost twenty-four years and feel very good about our relationship. Both of us were exposed to the teaching of the Bible as children and both of us made commitments of our lives to Jesus Christ. I'm convinced that the direction those commitments set for us, the people we became involved with, and the values we have drawn from the relationship had more to do with the quality of our marriage than any other factor. When a parent introduces his child to a vital Christian faith he is passing along to him the most precious gift of all.

For further thinking and discussion:

1. What values did you copy from seeing your parents act them out in life?
2. Do the people in your family know what the rules are? How were they made? How were they communicated?
3. Finish the sentence: My goal for my children is
_____.

4. Evaluate each of your children noting differences and similarities as it relates to both gifts and interest and the way each responds to correction.
5. Could there be a difference between the way a parent really feels about his children and the way the child thinks he feels?

5

Fathers Are Important

Fathers are more important than most people realize. Yet a father can be made to feel almost unneeded at times. With tongue in cheek Carlyle Marney suggested that at the time of a child's birth we fathers are considered biologically incidental. In early childhood we become economically necessary. It's only when the children reach adolescence and mother doesn't know what to do with them, that father becomes the responsible party for the whole affair. While Marney's statement was never meant as more than a caricature of the situation I understand the frustration which underlies it.

Children need fathers. A son needs a model for his life. A daughter needs a pattern for evaluating men. Billy Sunday, the famous evangelist, was wrong when he said in one of his messages, "Give a child a good mother and any old stick will do for a dad." All those mothers who are attempting to rear children without a father in the home will bear witness to how much both boys and girls need a father.

In one of his books on the family, Cecil Myers tells the story of the Washington, D.C., psychiatrist who was approached by a high government official. The man was so involved in the affairs of state that he didn't have time to be with his two sons. His proposition to the psychiatrist was unique. The official wanted the doctor to close his considerable practice and devote his full time to "fathering" his two sons. "I'm too busy with the needs of the country," he said, "and I know that you understand their needs. Money is no object." The psychiatrist graciously declined the offer and reminded the parent that there really is no adequate substitute for a father.

The government official's request does not seem so strange when we realize that there are actually individuals thinking and writing about the family who are suggesting such an alternative. Recently I read a serious paper written by a psychologist in which he was suggesting the emergence of what he called a "third parent" in the family to assume many of the responsibilities of the father. This "third parent" would be hired by the real father as evidence of his latent desire to provide for his son a truly committed paternal presence. While the entire article was written in the flawless jargon of psychology, it sounded for all the world like a commercial for "Hertz rent-a-dad." There is no effective substitute for fathers.

Jesus showed an awareness of the role of the father in the home. In one of his talks he was trying to emphasize the heavenly Father's interest in the needs of his children. He said, "If you, then, bad as you are, know how to give your children what is good for them, how much more . . . your heavenly father . . ." (Matt. 7:11). The inference was that even those of us who are not perfect still have it in our hearts to do what is best for our children.

What are the things your children need from you as their father? It is assumed that they need to be provided the physical necessities of life and that they need to be given whatever protection is necessary. Beyond these what do they really want and need from you as a father?

Love and Affection

Children need a father's love and affection. It needs to be both articulated and demonstrated. This is a need which continues throughout life. Whether you are dealing with a baby who needs burping after its bottle, a school child needing approval for a notebook with a large "A" marked on it, or a lanky teenager telling you he is hungry again, there is that continuing need the child has to know his father loves him.

Expressing love and affection is not easy for some men. There are men who feel deeply about their children but find it difficult to verbalize their love or show it emotionally. Part of this could be connected with the difference between the physical and emotional makeup of men and women. But much of it comes from cultural conditioning which starts when we are small children. Often I have been in a home where a death has occurred and there are small children who are beginning to grieve the loss of a parent or grandparent. Many times I have overheard some well-meaning father saying to a little boy whose heart is broken, "Don't cry now. Be strong. Be a little man." After years of that kind of conditioning it's not surprising that many men associate the showing of their feelings with weakness. But our need to express love is as great as our children's need to hear it.

Several years ago there was a delightful play called "Fanny" on Broadway. "Fanny" was the story of a young girl in love with a young man. When she told

him that she was pregnant his response was to take a
job on a ship and go to sea. There was another man
who knew all about the situation and was moved to
help. He married the pregnant girl and took care of her.
When the child was born it was given his name. Not
long afterward the young sailor came back into port
and discovered what had happened. He was furious,
and he wanted "his" baby. In discussing the situation
with an uncle he sought to state his case for custody of
the child.

"Tell me, uncle. Who is the real father? The one who
gave the baby life or the one who buys its bibs?"

The uncle's simple reply was, "The father is the one
who loves."

How does a father show his love for his children?
The most obvious way is with words. Get into the
habit of telling your children that you love them. Speak
to your wife about your feelings for the children. In
talking to friends and relatives about your children
don't be reluctant to tell others of your love. It may
be a simple, "I love you," as you tuck a youngster into
bed or a reassuring, "Your mother and I love you very
much," when one of your teenagers is having a difficult
time.

If the words don't come easy then write them. For
several years my work involved being out of town
more than was healthy for my family. I began writing
little stories for my daughter and mailing them home.
I printed them so they would be easy to read and drew
little pictures throughout for her to color. In terms of
literary value I doubt they will ever replace any of
the classics, but it gave me a way of saying "I love you"
to a little girl who was several hundred miles away but
very much in my thoughts. That little girl is now
twenty-one and in law school. Sometimes I still tell her
my feelings in writing.

A father needs to show his love by touching his children. Everyone knows how vital it is for a baby to be held, to be touched, and to feel love. This is a need none of us really outgrows. The need to be touched is as vital for young boys as for young girls. This is why I find it strange that a man will hug his daughter but shake hands with her younger brother. While their growth soon makes it difficult to hold them in your lap, boys continue to need some physical expression of love and affection.

Sometimes you act out your love by doing something very special for your child. For me the one relaxed morning of the week is Saturday. Several years ago I noticed a recipe in the paper for French pancakes. It seemed simple enough for my somewhat limited abilities in the kitchen and it sounded good. So the next Saturday morning I tried them on the family as each one got up and came to breakfast. Though everyone did something different with the pancakes, they all liked them. Ever since then Saturday and French pancakes have gone together at our house. And there are times when I think if pancakes could talk they might say, "Your daddy loves you."

Recently I saw a little plaque hanging on a wall. It said, "The best thing a father can do for his children is love their mother." That's good. But beyond that, he needs to love his children and express that love.

Children Need Boundaries

Another thing a father needs to do for his children is to define the boundaries for their young lives. Children need limits. These boundaries need to be arrived at with wisdom and they need to be communicated with love and firmness. Children are not simply shorter adults. They are children. If they are to know who they are, feel loved, and learn how to function, they need a sense of stability and security. Once the structures are established and the child understands them, he feels more secure.

Firmness is not the same as rigidity, and exercising authority is not the same as being authoritarian. Most of us have heard some version of the story about the man who came out of the army after a highly successful career. He married and decided the best way to "run" his family was according to the military system. His children were awakened by reveille and before breakfast were lined up to stand inspection. After one particularly complicated explanation of the "orders for the day" the father asked, "Are there any questions?" His youngest son's reply was, "Yes, how does one transfer out of this chicken outfit?"

While there is a great difference between a family and a military unit, a family does need rules. All families have them. Sometimes they're verbalized and sometimes they aren't. Certain families have too many rules and some too few. These rules set the boundaries. They have to do with everything: how people are treated, behavior at meal time, use of the car, when to come in at night, and a host of other things. Rules are absolutely essential if a family is to function efficiently.

While a family requires a great deal of flexibility, at the core there needs to be some rules which are not negotiable. These need to be understood and enforced. Another group of rules should be negotiated as ages change and growth and maturity take place. A father who is fair and firm in defining and applying the rules of the family will be meeting a real need in his children.

Fathers Need to Know

It is important for children to know that their father is aware of their growth and development. How easy it is to become so involved with one's career and the overall responsibilities of rearing a family that the children grow up and leave us without our being aware of it! One of my favorite musicals of all time is "Fiddler on the Roof." Much of the plot and the music revolve around the family. One of the real tensions in the musical comes because Tevia, the father in the house, had not realized how much his children were changing in their ideas and attitudes as they grew up. He just assumed that tradition would go on unchanged generation after generation.

One of the tenderest scenes in the musical comes when, at the wedding of their daughter, Tevia and his wife sing "Sunrise, Sunset." The whole of the parents' emotions are summed up in the lyrics, "I don't remember growing older, when did she?"

Children do grow. Growth is rapid and irreversible. When they are little with no embarrassment they cry to you, "See how I've grown." As they grow older they are reluctant to call attention to their development—but they want you to notice anyway.

Being aware of their growth and development will make it easier to understand them, appreciate them, and communicate with them. A father needs to be aware of how his children are doing in school, who their friends are, their latest interest, and the changes taking place in their lives. This doesn't require hiring a private detective but it is information readily available by listening to and watching the children. And you may want to ask for a little help from your wife!

It is of great importance to try to keep in touch with the feelings of your children. Sometimes they're hurt, sometimes angry, sometimes lonely, sometimes sad. Sometimes these feelings are verbalized and sometimes they are communicated nonverbally. It is important for the message to get across. Sometimes it doesn't and the results are disastrous. One day a man came to me very distressed because there had been a complete breakdown of communications with his son. The boy had moved out of the house, quit school, taken a job, and refused to talk with his father. The father seemed to be taken completely by surprise by his son's move. Since I did not know the man or his family I decided to visit with some of the families who were close friends. Almost every individual I talked to said, "I've been watching this boy store up anger against his father for years." It seems that no one was surprised but the father. Had he kept in touch with the feelings of his son he could have dealt with the anger when it was a small thing.

Fathers Are Human

A father needs to be willing to be finite and mortal in his children's eyes. The first emotions a child feels toward a father are that he knows everything and can do anything he wants. Somehow the tiny child does not associate finiteness with either of his parents, but especially is this true of his attitude toward his father.

I remember how hard on me it was to discover that my father was like me. Our family lived on a small farm and was very poor. We had a garden for vegetables, chickens for eggs and meat, and a cow for milk. The most valuable things we owned were the two horses with which my father worked the place. One of the horses became ill and died suddenly. There was no way for me to know at such a young age what a blow this was to my father. What I remember was coming up behind him in the barn and discovering that he was crying. That's the first time I remember being aware that fathers could be hurt and not know what to do. It made me sad and I never talked to anyone about it.

Now I've come to discover how very important it is for a father to be willing to admit that he is neither omniscient nor omnipotent. This will not lessen the love or respect your children will have for you. In many cases it makes it possible for fathers and their children to be closer. The image which needs to be shattered is that fathers are the ones who know all the answers, can take charge in all situations, are always right, and never make mistakes. What needs to be communicated is that fathers *do* have great responsibility in the home but that it is possible for fathers to misunderstand a situation, to make wrong judgments, to get their own egos involved in a situation, and to need forgiveness.

There will be times when you will need the forgiveness of your child for something you've said or done. It is not an easy thing to be by yourself with a son or daughter and say, "I was wrong. I wasn't really listening and didn't understand. It was my fault and I'm sorry. I've asked God to forgive me and now I'm asking you." Knowing what kind of courage such a confession takes, a child would be very proud to have such a father.

The child who gets to know and love and respect father as a human being will have a much easier time relating honestly to his/her own children after marriage.

Fathers Are Leaders

There is a whole family of needs which a child has in relation to his father. These can best be labeled "leadership." The Bible's portrait of the father is always as leader. Lives which are worth living need goals and directions and some basic attitudes. Children need to feel that their father is leading the family in the direction which is best.

There's a kind of leadership which a man gives the

children by the way he relates to his work. We no longer live in the kind of world where a man's sons are his apprentices and are brought up in his trade. But we do live in a world where certain wholesome attitudes about work need to be learned. If a man's work comes across as drudgery then his children are apt to think all work is unrewarding and unfulfilling. No experience equips children with a wholesome attitude toward work like a father who finds meaning in what he's doing and shares that excitement with his children.

The father's leadership is most critical in moral and spiritual matters. Children learn respect for people, respect for property, and respect for themselves from watching their fathers in action. Nothing is more frustrating for a child than to be taught one set of values by his father and to see a different set of values operative in his life. Children will more often copy what they see than what they hear.

Nothing will build character in a child more solidly than seeing values in action. William Hall Preston is a man whom I've admired for many years. I've known his children since they were in college. My wife worked in his office for a while in Nashville. I often visit with him when he and his wife are in Houston. Last year, nearing his seventieth birthday, he wrote a book entitled *Fathers Are Special*. Since I had observed him to be a real super-father I anticipated that the book might be his own philosophy about fathers. Instead it was mainly about his father whom I had never met.

In the book he talks about his father's integrity. Then he records the incident in his life which had communicated that virtue. His father had a cast-iron stove for sale. Some people came to look at it and after a casual inspection of the stove, were about to buy it. Before taking their money his father asked, "I'm sure you noticed the little hole on the side?" They hadn't and, as a result, didn't buy the stove. More than sixty years later William Hall associated honesty with what he had seen his father do in that simple experience.

Children need to see fathers leading in the area of religious development and commitment. A father's religion demands an outward expression. Children must see their father as a worshiper and as a believer. A father's religion should be woven naturally into the many relationships in the family.

Available and Accessible

A father needs to be available and accessible to his children. Children require time with us. I have a friend who is one of the outstanding educator/counselors in the country. We were discussing the demands of our respective jobs one day and the effect this was having on our relationship with our children. He laughingly remarked to me, "Yes, Ken, I know about that. Recently I looked down at the schedule of people my secretary had made appointments for me to see and discovered my youngest son's name. When he came in I half expected him to come up with some big problem he was having which he might be reluctant to discuss at home with his mother. That wasn't it at all. He had absolutely no agenda. He just wanted to visit with me."

As I replayed the conversation with my friend, I realized that his son was really no different than any other child in his desire to be with his dad. Those of us who are fathers need to face realistically the fact that it is not possible to spend as much time with our children as we might like. But if we decide to use well the time we do have with our children, it can have a tremendous impact upon their lives.

When I was in the fourth grade both of my parents

had already left for work when I started for school. And they had not yet returned when I came home again. In addition to this they often had to work a half day on Saturday. Yet I have happy memories of being with my parents during this period of my life. I can still remember visiting with relatives, all-day fishing expeditions, and trips back to Oklahoma which seemed like great adventures. The quality of the time we spend with our children may be more important than the quantity.

One reason we need nonstructured time with our children is that it creates a better climate for listening and talking. It would be ideal if our children would come in and ask all their difficult questions immediately after we have attended a seminar on "hard questions your children are about to ask." But it doesn't happen that way! Those moments of interest and openness and seriousness with children seem always to come in some unexpected context. And after they're over you say to yourself, "I wouldn't have missed the opportunity of that conversation for anything." Then you realize that this kind of communication takes place only when you're together.

Nathan and Fran live in Arkansas, but he used to be a member of my staff in Atlanta. An exciting speaker, he usually focused his ministry on students. His speaking engagements took him away from home almost every weekend. Even when he was in town he was constantly being asked to speak to various groups during the week.

He came into my office one day with a big smile on his face and announced, "Well, I'm back in the picture." I didn't have the slightest idea of what he was talking about so I asked him to explain. This was his explanation:

"Six months ago I was sitting at the table one night. During the meal I asked my daughter what she had done at school that day. She was glad for my question because it gave her an opportunity to show me a picture she had drawn for which she had received an 'A.' It was a picture of our family.

"When I looked at the picture I discovered, to my shock and amazement, that I wasn't in it. It was a picture of Fran and the children. Even my daughter was not aware that I was not in the picture until I called her attention to it.

"That was six months ago. Since then I have consciously tried to spend more time with my children. But more than anything else, I've tried to really be with them when I'm home.

"The reason I'm so happy is that this week my daughter did another picture of our family and I'm in it."

When I was a professor in the seminary in Ft. Worth, our oldest daughter, Nancy, was a preschooler. One night I came home just to get a bit of supper before returning to the school to speak to a group of parents on the assigned subject, "The Christian Father."

We had hardly begun supper before Nancy inquired whether or not I was going to be home all evening. She seemed very disappointed when I told her I had to return to the school to speak that night. To take the edge off her disappointment, I decided to ask her if she would like to help me with my talk. I told her I was going to be speaking about daddies and asked if she would like to help me make a list of what a good daddy would do. I got a piece of paper and a pencil and laid it beside my plate. All during the meal she kept thinking of things. Each time a new idea came along she would get down off her chair and whisper it in my ear. Then I would write it down.

When I returned to school, while they were introducing me to speak, I looked down at the list and it went like this:

1. Can catch a fish.
2. Can fly a kite.
3. Can build a fire.
4. Can catch a butterfly.
5. Can plant a flower.
6. Can get a kitty-cat out of the mud.

The list went on. Looking at the list my first thought was that almost everything on the list was something she had seen me do. Then the impact of the list really hit me. Nothing on the list required me to buy her anything—but everything on the list required me! Perhaps the thing a child needs most is for the father to be available.

For further thinking and discussion:

1. Was it easy or difficult for your father to express love?
2. What are some of the nonnegotiable rules at your house?
3. Do your children communicate their feelings to you? How?
4. Did your father ever let you see him as human?
5. What are the best times you have with your children each week?
6. Could you articulate your family's goals to your children?

6

Mothers Are Essential

When you say "mother" to a little child, he usually thinks of her functions first, then her feelings. "She feeds me and cleans the house" would probably precede, "She loves me."

But as we grow to adulthood our minds become a thick album of pictures which are all associated with the word mother. One of the first to come to our consciousness is a picture of our own mothers. My mother is now almost seventy years old and lives in Illinois near my two younger brothers. She lives in her own house and with a little help from my brothers for the heavier work, still has the best garden and the most beautiful flowers of any of us. Like many mothers one of her favorite activities is feeding her children. Fixed in my mind is the look of satisfaction on her face last fall when all of her grown children were in her house around her table eating and, in between helpings, assuring her that she had not lost her touch.

Strong in my mind is a picture of a new mother being checked out of the hospital in which her baby was born. I can identify with the father, who up to now hasn't even been allowed to hold the baby, but who is now feeling a little more needed as he orchestrates the transition from hospital to home. The memorable part of this picture to me is the look on the young mother's face as she holds her first child securely in her arms. She looks so much more mature than when she was checked in. There is a sense of awe that she has had a part in bringing a new life into the world and that the baby in her arms is an assurance of the future.

Another picture tugs at my heart. It is the memory of walking from the cemetery with a man who had just buried his mother. We walked along in silence, each with his own thoughts, and I felt with him the kind of loneliness that comes from giving up the one who brought you into the world.

The picture which sparks my curiosity is the one I get when I peek out from the little side room to see if the ushers have seated the mother of the bride. That signals the beginning of the wedding. I see her sitting there and, watching her expression as her own daughter comes down the aisle, I wonder what she is thinking. I've thought of having copies of Ruth Bell Graham's poem printed and giving one to her as a prayer.

> May she have daughters
> of her own
> to care
> when she is old
> and I am gone.
> I should have loved
> to care for her once more
> as I did then
> long years before.
> I was a mother young
> and she—my child.
> Caring was joy. So when

100

she is old and I am There,
may she have daughters
of her own
to care.*

Any book on the family would have to give promi-
nence to the role of the mother. As you have read the
first five chapters of this book you have noticed that
the woman, both as wife and mother, plays a significant part. She is 50 percent of the chapter on the
couple and carried more than half the load in the
parenting chapter. She figures prominently in all the
pictures of the family and in facing the problems confronting the family. Not one of the things children need
from a father is omitted from the list of what they
need from a mother.

Consequently in this brief chapter we are going to
deal with some of the needs of mothers and some of
the very special needs met by the mother. In addition,
I want us to take a look at the way the feminist movement is affecting ideas about mothering and also consider how working mothers can be most helpful to
their children.

Mothers Have Needs

We usually think of a mother as meeting the needs
of the other persons in the family because that is what
she is doing most of the time. But mothers have needs
which must be met if they are to continue to be effective in their role. These needs grow out of the fact
that she plays many roles in the family: woman, wife,
mother.

First, she is a woman. Her sense of personhood comes
from this. As a woman her most basic need is for self-

---

* From *Sitting by My Laughing Fire* by Ruth Bell Graham (Waco:
WORD, 1977) p. 167. Used by permission.

esteem. She needs to feel that she has worth as a person, that she is valuable, that she is special. The love, support, and appreciation she receives from her husband and children are important in relation to how she sees herself. The fatigued mother cried, "I've cooked so many meals and washed so many clothes that I wouldn't be a bit surprised to look into the mirror some morning and discover I had turned into an appliance." This is just another way of saying that she doesn't feel like a person but like a function.

All the persons in the family need an opportunity to grow and develop as persons, even mothers. The picture of a mother without interests is a picture of an uninteresting mother. The mother who does not have the opportunity to develop and grow as a person will not be able to do the best job of either nurturing her marriage or guiding the growth and development of her children.

Second, she is a wife. She became a wife before she became a mother and those first needs do not stop once children are born and more of her time is devoted to their care. After the birth of children in some marriages the husband turns to his career to meet his needs and the wife tries to meet her needs in her children. This is not good for the children, for they deserve two parents and not one, and it will spell disaster to the marriage. The importance of the husband and wife meeting each other's needs in the marriage relationship has already been emphasized in the chapter on "The Marital Pair."

Third, she is a mother. This is not her whole identity. It is simply the name given one of her functions. In this role she has many needs. Often she has real doubts about her effectiveness. A friend whom I know to be an excellent mother told me that one of her constant frustrations as a mother had been that almost every time she picked up a magazine there would be an article in it written by some expert about what to do to be a good parent. She said the articles invariably covered a period in life which her children had already experienced. When she read the article and realized all the things she had done wrong, according to the expert, she would become depressed and feel like a failure. "One day," she said, "I made a decision about all those articles. I decided that since I was doing the very best I could and my children knew I loved them, that would just have to do."

Mothering is only one side of parenting. The other side is fathering. More and more I am coming to believe that those of us who are fathers need to play a larger part in the parenting process. Years ago when I would hear a speech on mothers I was always prepared for the long list of quotes from prominent people in our society telling how their mothers were instrumental in their success. I didn't doubt the evaluation and just accepted it as the way things are. Then I began to wonder if this is the way God intended it to be. I feel God gave children two parents because they need two parents to equip them for life. I'm not sure the system we've worked out is either right or healthy for the children. One of the big functions fathers have is to be more active partners in the important business of parenting.

Mothers Meet Needs

The needs which are met in a family by the mother are as diverse as life itself. Sometimes the people whose needs she meets are the least aware of all she does. An eager young mother with children in elementary school read an article which impressed upon her how important it was to spend time with her children when they came home from school. This seemed right and wise to her so to make that time she pushed herself during the day to get all the cleaning, cooking, shopping, and other responsibilities out of the way. Then she could devote herself to the children when they arrived home.

Everything went along well and she felt good about the sacrifice she was making to be available to her children. The good feeling left her completely one day when her son brought home a paper which he had written concerning what mothers do. In the paper he had said that his mother didn't do anything but watch television with him, play games, and have parties. Then and there she decided that when the children came home they would have opportunity to see her cleaning the house, cooking supper, and a few of the other things which mothers did!

A mother meets the needs of her children by modeling her role as woman and mother. To her son she begins as the most important woman in his life. A son will resist to the death any effort his mother makes to interest him in some young lady she likes and would probably resent any suggestion as to the kind of person he ought to marry. But his mother is the one by whom he judges the girl he will marry. While a son has been known to pick a wife who is the opposite of his mother, most of the time he looks for those qualities he has come to appreciate in her.

The mother plays a similarly important role with her daughter. From her mother she receives an understanding not only of what it means to be a person but to be a woman.

In hundreds of ways as the children are growing up the mother teaches principles for living as a part of the concrete experiences of life. When a mother cut a vein in her arm while working in the kitchen, she stopped the bleeding momentarily by wrapping a towel around it. Holding the towel over the cut she walked into the den, told her teenage daughter what she had done, and asked the girl to drive her to the emergency room of the hospital to have the injury cared for.

The doctors stopped the bleeding, sewed up the cut, bandaged it, and gave the mother a tetanus booster shot. After this the daughter, who had been quite shaken by the whole affair, took her mother home. On the way she asked with awe in her voice, "How were you able to stay so calm?" The mother explained to her that when something bad happens all panic does is to keep a person from taking care of the problem.

In sharing the incident with me, the mother said that she had overheard her daughter talking about what had happened and especially emphasizing how calm her mother was. There's a chance that the daughter may go through life without ever seriously cutting herself, but when something bad happens and everyone else is losing his head there's a possibility that she will be the one who stays calm and becomes a part of the solution. The daughter learned the principle in an unforgettable way.

Children need big ideas like love translated into terms they can understand. One of the simplest and most meaningful ways a mother does this is by being sensitive to the differences in the personalities and needs of her children. She shops with them for curtains for their room and listens as they express preferences. A mother notices the length young men are wearing their jeans and the kind of socks girls are wearing in junior high. She spends time alone with each of her children, but she is also sensitive to their need for privacy and quiet times. Every day the children are learning about a very special kind of love woven into the fabric of life by their mother. Mothers are specialists at meeting the needs of children.

Mothers play a special role in the religious development of their children. All the foundations for adult faith are laid in the simple experiences of childhood, most of which take place in the home. As the child becomes aware of himself he can be told of God's love for him which does not change. As the child becomes aware of the world with all its beauty and mystery he can learn that it is good because God made it. All the relationships which involve trust, love, and even forgiveness can give meaning to ideas which will someday equip the child for a vital faith. The words which he hears in church about God's love will only have meaning if he has had experiences which actualize it in the home.

There are certain special contributions that mothers make which enrich the larger viewpoint of the children. Mothers seem to have an elemental sense of judgment and compassion, an unusual capacity for selflessness. They can project and identify with others. Their faith in God may not be more profound than that of others but it seems more intimate. These qualities complement those of the husband and enrich the family.

Mothers and Women's Lib

The mother is the only member of the family who is having to define her role in the midst of a revolution. The whole feminist movement has stirred deep emotions about the identity of women and the role of the mother. Most of the media coverage is being given to the statements and actions of leaders on the extreme left or right of the issue. But the really significant thing is that the middle is being moved. Women who wouldn't be caught dead at an Equal Rights Amendment rally, pro or con, are changing the way they see themselves and are rethinking their role in society and in the family. The degree to which this is happening was dramatized for me recently when a little eight-year-old girl asked, "Since Jesus chose twelve apostles why didn't he choose any women?"

When the whole woman's liberation movement, in its current form, burst on the scene and began to capture the imagination of women and the attention of our society, there were some frightening implications for the family. While the frustration and anger of the early leaders is understandable, the intensity of the hostility which was focused on the idea of having babies and mothering shook many people. Many knowledgable people now feel that as the awareness of the worth and the needs of women is heightened a certain amount of moderation will take place within the movement itself.

Already there is the hint that the movement is changing in its criticism of the family. Probably we will see more of a focus on the importance of the role of the mother with the children. If this happens then we may see more and more women exercise the choice which they have in favor of having children and being mother to them. These women who had other options and chose to become mothers will bring a superior quality of commitment to their marriage and to their children.

Women Have Choices

For many reasons today's women have choices which their mothers and grandmothers did not have.

They can stay single if they choose because they are no longer dependent upon marriage for financial support. Or they can delay getting married if they choose. This gives them the opportunity to work for a while and grow up a bit before entering into a marriage. This may help those women who otherwise would move from their father's house to the interdependent relationship with their husband without any time in between to be independent.

Women have greater choice about having children and about the timing of the birth of their children. This has tended to extend the period between the beginning of the marriage and the birth of the first child. Often this is a big help in allowing the couple time to begin adjusting to each other and to begin seriously nurturing the relationship they have as husband and wife.

More today than at any other time the option of either devoting themselves full time to homemaking or working outside the home is open to mothers. For some this is not an option. Because of the ages of their children and the nature of the husband's job and its demands, some mothers would find it impossible to work outside the home without abandoning the family. Likewise, there are a large number of mothers who must for financial reasons work at a job outside the home. This would include all the parents who have sole responsibility for their family and an increasing number of wives whose extra income is made necessary by inflation, heavier taxation, and the increased cost of education for the children.

But there is an increasing number who do have choices. Some are choosing one way and some another. I watch a number of mothers go to work because they are sensitive to needs in the community and feel they ought to play a part in meeting them. If it were not for this fact the public school system would fold immediately. Some of the best trained, most caring, and most capable women in our society are teaching school under difficult circumstances for poor pay because they have a sense of mission and are fulfilling it in that way.

I have a friend who has always had an eye for needs in the community and has done something about it. Recently she moved to another town. One day she returned for a visit and we were discussing her new home town. She said, "The women in my neighborhood mystify me with the way they spend their time. There are so many needs among the people which they could meet so easily. But here are these well-educated, wealthy, talented women who play tennis all morning, have lunch at the club, and then play bridge until time for the children to come home." As she shook her head back and forth she concluded, "What a waste!"

I know of mothers who go to work because they have talents and gifts and abilities. They would not be happy if they were not using the gifts in helpful ways. Others go to work because they have a strong need to be around other people and to meet new people.

In a way those of us who have spoken to the whole matter of the working mother have tended to miss the issue. It may not be a choice between working or not working. It may be the need to stay alive and to keep developing as a person. The issue is the need to stay interested in things and to stay interesting to your spouse, your children, and yourself.

For years one of my favorite passages in the Bible modeling the ideal for mothers was Proverbs 31:10–31. Somehow in all the times I had read that passage I thought of the mother as a woman who took care of her house and children while her husband sat at the gate. Recently I was forced to look at those same verses through the eyes of women and discovered that this was a very interesting, alive, alert, and enterprising woman. While she took good care of all the needs of her household she was also involved in several profitable businesses and had even bought a piece of land with her own money and planted a vineyard. You might be as amazed as I was if you were to read this short passage in that light.

Women who choose to work outside the home do not seem to cripple their children if they have the support of their family in their efforts. There are even some indications that these children develop independence and self-sufficiency at an earlier age. The important thing in every case seems to be the children's knowledge that even though the mother is working outside the home the family still has top priority with the parents.

An increasing number of mothers with choices are deciding to devote themselves exclusively to their homes. In days past the pressure was for women to stay home. That has now been reversed. Today those who stay home are the ones who feel the need to explain. Recently I was visiting a young woman who, with clear goals and well-thought-through commitment, had decided to devote full time to homemaking. But so many of her age group who were married and had children were working that she expressed the wish that these friends "wouldn't be too quick to judge me for my decision."

What encouraged me was that she had a choice. She had made a good decision and was finding stimulation and fulfillment in what she was doing.

Having choices eventually means there will be happier, more satisfied mothers in the home and that will mean happier children and husbands.

For further thinking and discussion:

1. What were the most important things you learned from your mother? How were they taught?
2. Will the fact that women have more options eventually strengthen or weaken the home?
3. What are some of the qualities mothers bring to the family which are unique to her as a woman?
4. Do you think all women are seeing themselves differently today? How is this being expressed?
5. Could you explain to your daughter or son the needs a woman has as a person, as a wife, and as a mother?

7

Listen to the Children

You would be absolutely amazed, and probably comforted, if you knew what your children think about your family. Two years ago I was invited to visit each of the children's departments in our church "so the children will get to know you better." I accepted the invitation but with the clear intention to use the occasion to get to know *them* better. Each group usually met me at the door with a nametag, often a "Welcome Dr. Chafin" speech, and an invitation to have a seat and "talk" to them. I worked out a little routine in which I would try to accomplish several things in the few minutes I was with them. I wasn't too experienced at communicating with small children and they weren't too experienced at paying attention for a long time.

Two of the things I did were real eye-openers to me. First, I agreed to answer any question they asked. They wrote out questions ahead of time, or asked the teacher to write them if they couldn't. Their questions were so sharp and so penetrating that they forced me to rethink my whole approach to communicating with children.

The second thing I did was to ask the children to evaluate the church's worship service, item by item. It was devastating! Most of us who are adult, in spite of the fact that we were once children, tend to forget how straightforward and honest youngsters can be. I listened to them talk about the music. They asked questions about the offering. Then we came to the sermon. Normally I speak about twenty-five minutes. When I asked them how long they thought the sermon was, the shortest estimate I heard was "three hours."

After I had visited each of the children's departments I decided that it had been one of the really good experiences of my life. I discovered there is more to be gained from listening to children than many realize. When I began writing this book, I decided that in this chapter I would give the children an opportunity to speak to all of us about the family. It won't be too painful and it will be more reassuring to you as a parent than you can imagine.

What Children Think

To find out what the children were feeling and understanding about the family, a simple questionnaire was prepared and used with a hundred children from preschool through junior high. The ages covered a ten-year span, four to fourteen. Because our church has a large ministry with internationals and an outreach to neighborhood children, the group reflected a cross section of races, cultures, and educational levels. The children who could not yet read or write were interviewed by their teachers. The others wrote their own answers.

It was explained to each of the children that I was

writing a book on the family and wanted to know what they were thinking about some things. The following questions were given to each child:

1. What do you think a family is?
2. Who is in your family?
3. Why do you think we live in families?
4. What would it be like if people did not live in families?
5. What are mothers like? What are fathers like?
6. What are mothers for? What do they do?
7. What are fathers for? What do they do?
8. Who is the most important person in your family to you?
9. If you could change one thing in your family what would you change?
10. What does your family do together for fun?

The children split down the middle on how they answered the first question concerning what a family is. Half defined the family in terms of the functions it performs or the relationships which exist in the family. They defined the family as:

> A place that your mother and daddy feed you . . . . something with a mother and father and brothers and sisters . . . . people who live together . . . a group of people who are related . . . . mother, father, etc. . . . a woman, a man, a *dog*, a brother, and a sister . . . .

The other half of the group defined the family in terms of feeling. In answering question 3 ("Why do you think we live in families?"), with only a few exceptions all of them gave the purpose of the family in terms of need, support, love, and caring. Their idea of the purpose of the family was:

to take care of you . . . . people who live together
and love each other . . . . so we can learn . . . . to
take care of each other . . . . so we can help our whole
family . . . . a group of loving and caring people
. . . . it gives us a chance to tell our problems . . . .
because God wanted us to be able to look up to
parents . . . . need each other to help . . . . because
when you're little you can't do 'nothing' for yourself
. . . . to keep one another company . . . .

It is interesting that the children saw the family as
meeting both the emotional and physical needs of the
family members and in many cases listed spiritual
needs, learning needs, and needs relating to morality.
They *all* saw their parents as teachers.

The Importance of Families

The real surprise in the little questionnaire was the response to the question, "What would it be like if
people did not live in families?" This question more
than any other seemed to trigger the feelings of the
children. Having read their definition of the family as
being a place where love, care, and protection flour-
ished, it was easier for me to begin to grasp why it
was so frightening even to consider what would happen if they didn't have the family. They answered in
brief, emotionally packed words. The words most often
used were "lonely" and "sad." A partial list includes:

very sad	not good	no one to talk to
terrible	people would die	scattered
lonely	awful	no love
no help	mixed up	hard to live
not happy	boring	miserable
horrible	no special love	confusing
chaotic	a disaster	solitary

It is both interesting and rather reassuring that while there are so-called scholars writing books about the need for an alternative to the family, the children cannot even conceive of a world without families!

Mothers and Fathers

The most encouraging part of the answers came in response to questions 4, 5, and 6 which have to do with what mothers and fathers are like, what they're for, and what they do.

A few of the children described their mothers only in terms of the traditional functions she performs such as: "works, cleans house, cares for kids, helps with homework, feeds me, clothes me, stays home, does dishes, and has babies."

A few of the children described their mothers only in feeling terms such as: "nice, sweet, compassionate, teaches me, loves me, is warm, supports, kind, pretty, and comforts."

The most significant part of the response was that the overwhelming majority of the children described their mothers in both functional and feeling terms. Some examples are:

> She washes dishes . . . . she loves me.
> She cleans house . . . . she plays with me.
> She works . . . . she cares for me.
> She has babies . . . . she guides me.

The response concerning fathers revealed an almost identical balancing of the roles. Some defined him in traditional roles as the one who "makes money, goes to work, and fixes things." Others defined him in feeling roles such as: "teaches me right from wrong, is strong, is a friend, and loves me." Again the majority thought of their fathers both as doing certain things for them and also as relating to them as well. So the father:

> Works at the office . . . . plays with me.
> Makes money for our family . . . . loves me.
> Fixes things that break . . . teaches me.

It should be especially interesting to those fathers who have to be away from the home a lot to know that these children saw father as a friendly person who spends less time with them but has an extremely strong impact. While the mothers become the primary parent, especially for the babies, the older the child the more impact the father had. Part of the impact of the father may be connected to the fact that he *isn't* there all the time. This draws attention to the need to make the time spent with the children *quality* time.

We picked up one interesting note in question 8 which was, "Who is the most important person in your family to you?" As they did in the second question ("Who is in your family?"), many of the children listed pets as members of the family. These included dogs, cats, goldfish, and even one hermit crab. We were told the names of two of the dogs: Daisy and Buttercup. What was most interesting was not that the pets were important enough to the children for them to be listed as members of the family. Most interesting was that ten of the children listed pets as the most important *person* in their family to themselves.

When this fact was pointed out to a perceptive friend of mine, she suggested that the pets were chosen because they were probably the only member in the family less competent and more dependent than the child. The child was able to love them, care for them, feed them, "boss them," and cuddle them. In this way the child was developing parenting and nurturing skills.

The Most Important Person

In listing the most important person in the family, the rest of the children's choices reflected more their sex and age than anything else. As the girls grew older they saw the mother as more important. While the boys were more prone to list everyone as "most important," as they grew older they were less likely to list mother and more likely to list dad.

Everyone who read the responses was touched by the answers to question 9, "If you could change one thing about your family what would you change?" Twenty children left it blank indicating there was nothing they wanted to change. One boy, rather than leaving it blank, wrote, "I think my family is just right for me." Most of the changes suggested had to do with one of two situations: either something concerning discord in the family or family membership.

How to settle conflicts in the family seemed to be an important issue to the children. To these children the changes they would like to see had to do with:

> parents stop fighting
> parents have less arguments
> more patience
> less yelling
> brothers and sisters fighting.

Thirty children wanted to change something which had to do with family size or family membership. The emotions of the child are inescapable as they suggest changes:

> want brother to move back to Houston
> change sisters to brothers
> more kids in the family

want daddy back
want sister home from college
want mother to have a baby
less difference in age of kids
less kids in the family.

One interesting aspect of their response is that the departure of any member of the family, even to go to school, can cause a real crisis for a child.

We added one question for the junior high students only. It was, "Do you see your family differently now that you are an adolescent? In what ways?" There were the responses you might have expected. One girl said, "Now I see they (parents) are people, too, unlike before." But another girl complained, "Now I see they can make more mistakes than me." There was a crying out for relationship from a boy who gets up, goes to school, comes home, and does homework without any contact with any other member of his family. In reading the responses of the thirteen- and fourteen-year-olds, the majority felt that their family was more important to them now than before. The same idea was expressed many ways:

It is more important to me.
I realize that you need a family to look after you and help you.
Now that I'm older I see how important my family is.
I understand my family better and they understand me.
I see my family as people who love me and raise me right.
I understand their opinions better.
I can talk to them about my problems.
They talk to me more.
We are closer than before.
I am beginning to grow up a little.

As I read what teenagers were thinking about their families, I wondered if their parents had any idea what good feelings their kids had about their parents and families. Probably not. What more could a parent ask than to have a teenager say, "When I became an adolescent, I found out that not only was I a person, but so were mom and dad. They didn't seem quite so heartless or infallible."

If this little exercise in listening to the children has done nothing else, it ought to be a reminder of several things. First, children have many thoughts and feelings about the family and we should try in our families to find out what they are.

Second, the roles of mothers and fathers are not as confused in the minds of the children as in the minds of some adults.

Third, the traditional idea of the family as a man and woman who marry and have children is deeply embedded in the thinking of our children.

Fourth, children *do* look to their parents for the guidance which equips them for life.

For further thinking and discussion:

> 1. Get every member of your family to answer the questions on the questionnaire and then discuss the answers with each other.
> 2. Engage a child who is not a member of your immediate family in a discussion and listen to his thoughts about mothers, fathers, and families.
> 3. Since conflict is normal in a healthy family, how can it be handled in a way which is constructive for the whole family? Discuss with mate and children.

8

Sex in the Context of Love

Any discussion of sex in the context of the family needs to look at two areas: the sexual relationship of husband and wife and the sex education of the children. There is much interrelation and overlap in the two areas. Let's look at the children first.

It is a warm and delightful experience for parents to watch their sons and daughters as they begin to develop a sexual awareness. This awareness is a sign of passage from childhood to adulthood and it stirs mixed emotions. There is a gladness at their growth and maturing, and there is a tinge of sadness in realizing how soon they will be leaving the home.

Because we are with her almost constantly, we parents are often the last to notice that our daughter is suddenly "grown up." But the clues were there for the watching. She worked a little harder with her hair and started experimenting with eye shadow. A hint of shyness developed and, when with a group of girls, she giggled if boys were around. She developed an unbelievable crush on the lead trombone player in the band and he never knew about it. If accused of being interested in boys she would sometimes violently disagree. But the most noticeable thing was that when she walked she had that special "swish" which reminded you more of a woman than a little girl.

Boys reveal more obvious signs of sexual development. Often a little fuzz collects on the upper lip indicating that shaving will soon become necessary. Suddenly the little boy whose main motive for going camping was that he didn't have to take a bath becomes self-conscious about his looks, his clothes, the car, his brothers and sisters, and especially his parents. He begins looking at girls differently. Though he's embarrassed to discuss sex with his parents, he thinks about it a lot when he's alone and wonders what it's like.

As you watch your children cope with their emerging sexuality you know that it is just the beginning. Before long, after an all too brief time of maturing, they will be falling in love, becoming engaged, getting married, and beginning their own families. You can have warm feelings about that because it's the way God planned it. But right now, because you know a great deal more about what a powerful thing sex is, you have certain concerns for your children. As a result you begin to ask yourself some questions.

What attitudes do I want my sons or daughters to have about sex? This is an important question because one's attitude often controls one's understanding. Also there are so many attitudes toward sex that don't seem adequate or healthy.

In what context do I want my children to have intimate sexual experiences? Your daughter may be in school with girls whose mothers have asked the doctor to prescribe birth control pills for them. Your son may watch television programs which will suggest that having sexual intercourse with a girl when you are sixteen is a normal part of a healthy boy's sex education. I am quite aware both of the pressures which young people have on them and of the fact that different parents have different ideas as to how they should respond to these pressures. For me, marriage is the context in which sex will bring the greatest happiness. I will be discussing this later in the chapter. We must help our children establish some ideals concerning the context in which they will place sex in their lives.

How much do they need to understand about sex in order for it to have its proper place in their lives? This question is not so concerned about the physical aspects of the sex act itself. Young people can quickly find books and articles, even with pictures, to learn about that aspect of sex. But the larger understanding of sexuality is even more important to young people. So much of the contemporary writing and emphasis ignores the importance of love in sex.

What part can parents play in helping with attitudes, understanding, and ideals concerning sex? Merely contemplating the matter can be frightening to us parents. First, it forces us to do some rather heavy thinking about our own understanding of sex and our own sexual relationship. There are many things we feel strongly about which we have never organized enough in our minds to present with any understanding. Second, there is the big problem of communication. An effective dialogue with teenagers is often difficult on a simple subject. On the subject of the seriousness of sex merely putting it on the agenda might create panic. But the questions are valid and if we are able to think them through they may help us with our own understanding and maybe either now or later on with our children.

Sex Is Good

I've thought a great deal about the attitude which I want my children to have toward sex. At first I developed a long list of concerns, some of which were reflections of my fears for my children. After I thought through each of them, I decided I would settle for two basic attitudes. I would want my children to feel that sex is basically good. Also, I would like for them to think of sex as being very important. I believe that these two attitudes would be good foundations for understanding both the context and nature of the sexual relationship.

First, sex is good. A person is never going to experience meaningful sex if he believes that it is dirty or bad. The foundation for all our initial thinking about sex ought to be that it is good. Sex draws its goodness out of the fact that God created it. Looking at all he had created he said, "It is good."

Read the simple stories in the first two chapters of the Bible and several aspects of the origin of sex become clear. The whole idea of husbands and wives as partners who are created to meet each other's needs is evident in the verse, "Then the Lord said, 'It is not good for the man to be alone. I will provide a partner for him'" (Gen. 2:18). The creation story indicates that our maleness and femaleness come from God and that God gave his blessing to the couple with instructions to "be fruitful and increase" (Gen. 1:27–28). So the story of man's beginnings in the Bible has the basic couple entering into a sexual relationship from which came children. This is why sex ought not to be something to be embarrassed or ashamed about.

This positive attitude is in conflict with the Victorian notion that sex is sinful. Even though there has been a swing toward the idea that the body is good, there are many people still trapped by negative feelings about sex. I feel fortunate to have escaped from the early impressions I received about sex.

My earliest years were spent in a small rural community in northeastern Oklahoma. It probably wasn't too different from any other community during the early thirties of this century. Attitudes about sex were a hangover from that era when sex was treated as something so dirty it shouldn't be discussed. Most of us never heard an adult say the word until we joined an English class where they were discussing gender and then we were a little embarrassed.

We had a few cows. My father was so uncomfortable with any discussion of sexual matters around the children that when one of the cows was dry and needed to be bred, he would not even say the word "bull." He called it the "male cow"! To make matters even more confusing for curious children, when a calf came it was never referred to as having been born. Instead, my dad would tell the children that the cow had "found" a calf.

When my mother was pregnant no explanations were offered for the different shape of her figure. Although I overheard snatches of adult conversation which gave me hints as to what was about to happen at our house, I had the clear impression that these were things good little children didn't know about. When the time drew near for the baby to be born, we children were sent to stay with Aunt Ida and Uncle Parker. Then one day a postcard came with the announcement that we had a new little brother. I've always been thankful that the card didn't say that mother had "found" a baby!

One day years later, while I was a student at the University of New Mexico in Albuquerque, I went out to spend the afternoon with my Aunt Cora who lived by the river on Rio Grande Boulevard. At the time one of her daughters and her two sons were visiting. One of the boys was out with friends but Tommy, who had just started school, was there. My aunt had a beautiful female cat due to deliver kittens almost any day. Tommy was fascinated. I sat and listened with deep appreciation as his mother answered with accuracy and without embarrassment all the questions he asked about the birth of kittens. It seemed so natural and so right for this mother to communicate to her young son a wholesome attitude about sex.

Our children may get information from reading books and asking questions, but they pick up attitudes from watching us. A husband who comes into the kitchen and though his wife is up to her elbows in dish water, puts his arm around her waist and gives her a kiss on her perspiring cheek does not go unnoticed by children. A husband and wife who enjoy each other's presence send out happy signals that children pick up. If you and your mate feel that sex is a good thing then it would be almost impossible not to communicate this to your children.

Sex Is Important

The second attitude I would desire for my children is a feeling that sex is extremely important. Your first reaction may be that the opposite might be needed since ours is already being called a "sex-saturated society." Many people feel that since so many books, magazines, movies, television shows, and commercials are filled with sex, we need to de-emphasize sex. I had that same feeling until it was pointed out to me that the openness with which sex is being discussed is not the problem. The problem is the context it is being given.

If you will listen carefully to what is really being said and read between the lines of what is being written, you will discover an interesting phenomenon. Sex is being treated as a toy or a plaything. It is being looked upon as a recreational activity, like bowling. The very casual manner in which people who are almost strangers engage in sex has a way of saying, "It's no big deal." I had the whole philosophy articulated to me with great clarity by a high school student who said without any embarrassment, "It's like any other appetite. If I'm hungry I get a quarter-pounder with cheese, and if I want sex I get a girl who's willing."

Sex is too important a part of life to be reduced to destructive fun and games. It has tremendous potential for good but used carelessly it can be unbelievably disastrous. I would like for my children to have the feeling that while sex is good it is also extremely important and should be treated accordingly.

In addition to these attitudes I would like for my children to place sexual intercourse in the context of marriage. Sex needs the context of marriage to bring the joy, the ecstasy, the sense of well being, and the fulfillment it was intended to have. I'm convinced that this ideal was placed before us for our happiness. Ignoring the ideal brings unhappiness; striving toward the ideal brings joy. It's just that simple. This is not always easy for either young people or adults, but if we keep the ideal clear and strive toward it, we will find added strength. The advantages of sex within a good marriage as it relates to husband and wife will be discussed later in the chapter.

I've thought a great deal about the understanding I

would like for my children to have of sex. There are really two aspects. First comes the *physiological* aspects of sex. This usually starts with the question, "Where do babies come from?" and develops later into questions about all the physical aspects of sex. This is relatively simple. It can be done at school or at the YMCA or YWCA. It can come from checking out a book at the library. Wherever it comes from the information will usually be the same.

But the *relational* aspects of sex ought to be taught in the family. Only the family can adequately provide guidance in understanding the moral and emotional aspects of sex. This is the most important aspect of sex and it is an aspect too often ignored. I will be defining and illustrating this aspect of sex in the discussion of the husband-wife relationship.

Children will get a great deal of information and facts about sex outside the home. But they need to get their understanding of and attitudes toward the subject from the home. There needs to be developed the freedom to talk openly about sex at the level of the child's interest and awareness. A teenager will be more open in conversation if there has been openness about sex from the time he was small. A child will pick up many attitudes from watching his parents relate to each other, but there still needs to be verbal discussion.

There also needs to be some negative guidance, attitudes which ought not to be developed. Always there needs to be an effort to avoid creating fears in the mind that will extend into marriage. The previous generation may have made a mistake, for instance, in giving as the only reason for not engaging in premarital sex the possibility either of pregnancy or venereal diseases. There are positive reasons for high sexual ideals which also need to be emphasized.

Sex Is Relational

For a husband and wife sexual intercourse represents the physical action by which the most intimate of all relations is acted out. In this act there is both physical and emotional intimacy. During the past several years most of the best selling books on sex have tended to emphasize the physical aspects of the sex act almost to the exclusion of the emotional or love aspect. For this reason the books have become more and more "how to" books with about the same amount of awareness of the emotional context as one would expect from "Popular Mechanics" magazine. While the strictly physical part of sex is important, it is possible to get all the purely physical information needed from excellent books in print long before today's best sellers came on the market.

The emphasis most of us need to hear is that it is not the sex act which gives meaning to our relationship but it is the quality of the relationship which gives meaning to the sex act. You may recall an earlier discussion in which the importance of nurturing the husband-wife relationship was emphasized. All the work you do on your marriage relationship will help your sex life to be more meaningful for both you and your mate. The great majority of people with good relationships can have a satisfying sex life.

A key factor in the total marriage relationship is communication. Sex within a marriage has great potential for communicating the meanings of tenderness, caring, love, and commitment. Though there are times when sex has been used as a substitute for communication, at its best sex is an expression of everything good in the relationship.

Many of the sexual difficulties in a marriage can be

traced to a breakdown in communication. Many therapists, when approached by a couple having sexual problems, will begin immediately to see how well the couple is communicating.

The discussion of sex needs to be taken off the taboo list both for husband and wife and for the children. Many couples will communicate freely and openly at every other level of life but won't talk to each other about sex. If comfortable communication is established about sex, several good things happen. First, this allows a way to get all the assumptions about sex out in the open where they can be confronted. Second, it will keep the husband and wife from taking each other for granted in the relationship. Finally, it will give both husband and wife the chance to say what pleases them or doesn't, what is pleasant or distasteful, and what is most satisfying to them.

People who would take their love and caring into their sexual relationship should work to keep this aspect of their lives growing and alive. There are many ways to accomplish this. Respect one another's moods and feelings in bed as you would in other places. Don't ever use sex to get even with a mate. Make a continuing effort to please one another. Make sex a real partnership.

Most couples need to be reminded to bring not only love to the sexual relationship but patience and a sense of humor. Each person and each couple is truly unique and there is a uniqueness about their sexual relationship.

The Best Context

At several points in this book I have stated my feeling that sex needs to be set in the context of marriage to be most meaningful and satisfying. Recently a friend who knows that this is the way I feel asked me, "What do you really believe that sex in the context of marriage has going for it that the other kind doesn't?" I had never been asked that particular question so it took a bit of thinking.

First I needed to define the type of husband-wife relationship in which I thought sex had its greatest potential for joy, well-being, satisfaction, and fulfillment. It would be a relationship in which there was tenderness, caring, sharing, love, commitment, and permanence. This meant that I would not deal with the destructive things which could happen with sex in a bad marriage. I decided to answer the question from the viewpoint of a good marriage relationship, of the type most of us are capable of developing with effort.

The list I made is mine. You might want to eliminate some points or add some of your own. This is what I feel sex in the context of a good marriage has going for it that the other kind does not.

In marriage there is much more likelihood of bringing the experiences of the total person to the sex act, thereby enriching it. A married couple will have eaten breakfast and dinner together, talked with each other about their day, watched the news together, shared things out of the newspaper, read a letter from a parent, made a decision about car insurance, and worked out the schedule for a long weekend in the mountains. All these little experiences of life are brought to the sex act and become a part of the sharing.

The permanence of the marriage relationship allows for growth and maturing in sex. Intimate relationships, whether sexual or not, have beginnings which are followed by growth and maturing. In the process a level of trust develops which was not possible at first. This makes people free to really share. Temporary sexual relationships have too many beginnings and no permanence.

The good marriage brings so many rich experiences to the relationship that sex is still meaningful when the couple is older and may be physically less attractive.

Because the couple in the marriage relationship are faithful to each other they do not live with the constant feeling they are competing with every other man or woman around.

The marriage relationship accumulates shared experiences over the years. The memories of every couple are filled with a storehouse of incidents of all sorts which, when shared, speak to the specialness of the relationship. This broadens the relational potential of sex.

Sex within the context of a good marriage isn't the constant challenge to the ego which it would be outside the relationship. This frees the couple to be more playful, to be less serious, and to enjoy each other more.

Sex within the context of a good marriage doesn't have to constantly deal with guilt. The married couple can wake up in the morning knowing who they are and what their relationship is. This fosters a feeling of well-being and a sense of the rightness of the total relationship.

Centuries ago the writers of the Hebrew Wisdom literature celebrated the relationship of husband and wife with these words:

> Let your fountain, the wife of your youth,
> be blessed, rejoice in her,
> a lovely doe, a graceful hind, let her
> be your companion;
> you will at all times be bathed in her love,

and her love will continually wrap you round.
Wherever you turn, she will guide you;
when you lie in bed, she will watch over you,
and when you wake she will talk with you
(Prov. 5:18, 19).

For further thinking and discussion:

1. What role does good communication have in the sexual life of the husband and wife?
2. Notice the sexual emphases in the media this week. Is sex treated seriously or lightly?
3. Why is the family the best place for children to gain their understanding and attitudes about sex?
4. How important is the health of the whole marriage relationship to sex in the family?
5. How much verbal communication about sex was there in the family in which you were reared?

9

Healing Broken Relationships

Except for a death in the family nothing is more devastating than a divorce. Nothing stands in greater contrast to the happiness and fulfillment within a healthy marriage than the hurt and anger of a marriage which has failed. It seems almost paradoxical that the very relationship which has such potential for healing could leave such scars upon people.

I'm convinced that in spite of all the problems which marriage confronts in today's world, it is possible for people to know and experience a quality of relationship in marriage which is everything God intended when he established the home. My wife and I are working toward that kind of relationship.

For a long time I had been aware that many marriages were ending in divorce, but only in recent years have I realized what a devastating experience the breakdown of a marriage is to a large circle of individuals. While the interest focuses on the couple breaking up there are parents and brothers and sisters on both sides involved. There are also several sets of friends involved, and more affected than anyone else, the children. The death of a relationship is not a simple matter of two individuals going their own way. It is a major shock to the whole family system and deserves to be considered in that light.

There are few persons who have not been affected by a divorce either within the family or within a circle of friends. This fact alone has made it easier for those who are concerned to begin trying to help. It has also forced us to think more about how we are going to relate to those whose marriages have failed. Somehow we must come to a position in our feeling and thinking which does not add to the problem. We must use all the wonderful resources of the family to help.

Our church faced the same problem which a family faces on this issue a few years ago and we were forced to choose what role we would play. All churches are *pro*family and as a result they have not known how to deal with the fact that some marriages end in divorce. The tendency as a whole has been to ignore the problem with the hope that it would either go away or take care of itself. As a result most churches have not done a serious study of the Scriptures, examined their own feelings in the matter, or thought much about the needs of the individuals being wounded by divorce.

In the fall of 1973 our church had to face the issue head-on. It came to us because of our efforts to help singles. In a period of nine months we secured staff to work with singles, bought and renovated a two-story building next to the church, enlisted and trained seventy-five lay workers, and launched an effective ministry to singles. Suddenly we had hundreds of single adults involved in every aspect of the life of the church.

Our real surprise came when we had our big after-church entertainment for singles. People came by the office and asked questions like, "Will the nursery be open?" and "When the singles have their seminar will there be child care?" At this point we discovered that as many as four out of ten singles in our city had been married but were now single. We also learned that most of them had not had any help in dealing constructively with what had happened to them. In talking to these people it took no special insight to learn that they had been badly hurt and were a long way from being healed.

So our problem was not philosophical or theoretical. Standing in front of us were scores of men and women who had failed in the most primary of all human relationships and who were now asking us to help them. After weeks of thought and discussion and prayer we came to this conclusion:

It will not be our role to seek out those who are guilty and judge them. There are already plenty of people who worry about who is to blame. It will not be our role to discover who the innocent people are and fix for them a halo to wear. We decided that our role was to take those who were hurting and seek by love and acceptance to be a part of their healing and beginning again. We have spent the last five years doing just that and are almost daily reassured as to the rightness of our decision, for we have seen what a powerful force people who really care can be.

Whatever kind of family it is facing the reality of a divorce, the issue is essentially the same. It is not a time for dealing with what might have been or even what ought to have been. It is a time for deciding how you will deal with what is. The best position to take is that no matter what has happened, you intend to love and accept the person or persons involved and attempt to the best of your ability to be a part of the help. Unless you come to this point in your attitude toward divorce you will become a part of the problem.

Parents Who Care

While parents are quite aware of the important role they play in the lives of their young children, they sometimes forget that this role continues throughout the child's life into adulthood. I have seen the painful process by which teenagers begin declaring their independence and the strong desire married children have to make it on their own. This often leaves parents feeling that nothing they think or say makes any difference to their children. But it just isn't so. When the marriage of a child gets into trouble the tendency is to keep it from parents not only because the child wants to try to work things out on his own but because he doesn't want to risk the disapproval of parents.

Over the years I've sat with a score of men and women who, even though they were going through the most difficult experience of their lives, expressed concern about what this was going to do to their parents. I can still hear the grown man weeping as he said, "This is going to kill my mother." Still fresh in my mind is the remark of a beautiful young woman who said, "I just don't think I can face my father with this." There are few needs as strong when trouble comes as the need for the love and acceptance of parents. Because this is true it means that there is no place where there is greater potential for healing than in a family which loves and cares.

One of the first things parents need to do is to come to grips with their own feelings and emotions. And one of the first reactions which needs to be labeled and dealt with is pride. There is a natural tendency in each of us to ask, "What will people think?" Nothing would be more deadly to our children than to be given the impression that what others think is more important to us than what they are suffering.

One of the strongest emotions is a sense of guilt. This comes naturally. We have assumed responsibility for our children for such a large part of their lives. Then, too, society has tended to make those of us who are parents the scapegoats for everything which is wrong with the world. We've read too many quotes like "There are no bad children, just inadequate parents." Consequently we are bound to ask ourselves questions like "What did we do wrong?" or "What did we fail to do?" All parents do some things wrong. All parents fail to do some of the things they ought to be doing. But wallowing in a sense of guilt will make us sick and cripple our efforts to minister to our children.

Don't be surprised if you feel anger at what is happening. This is one of the emotions we feel most when we are absolutely helpless. You may even find yourself trying to play the martyr's role as you cry, "How could they do this to me?" Sorting out all these feelings and admitting to yourself what they are will help keep them from being destructive.

It is normal for parents who love their children to hurt for them. This kind of empathy is a good common ground on which a husband and wife can build support for the children. It is of great importance that husband and wife, as a pair, deal with the problem. Because men and women are different, and because fathers and mothers have had different roles in relationship to the children, there is always the danger that a husband and wife will be in conflict over the issue. If this conflict is not confronted, rather than helping the child whose marriage has failed, you will find problems being created in your own marriage. Because the two of you need to be a team in helping your child, the worst thing you could do would be to take your frustrations out on each other. Share your feelings and your thoughts with each other and find a unity in your desire to help. One of the good things which can be salvaged from a bad situation is that your relationship could be strengthened by the way in which you deal with this problem.

What a Divorce Does to a Person

If more people understood what a divorce does to the persons going through it, they would react differently to people whose marriages fail. The best analogy I know is that divorce is like a death in the family. Instead of a physical death it is the death of the deepest of all human relationships, marriage. All the pain and all the emotions present where physical death has taken place are involved. I have been with men and women at the time they lost their mate by death and have observed what this loss does to them physically and emotionally. I've sat with people after the death of a marriage and discovered almost identical reactions to this different kind of death.

There is one sad difference between physical death and the death of a marriage. The family, the community, and the church know how to move in where someone has died and minister to those who grieve. When the time is near, the family and friends gather so we will not face the loss alone. After the death friends and neighbors come with words of concern, food for the table, and arms which embrace us.

The visitation at the funeral home, the memorial

service, and even the trip to the cemetery are a part of the way in which we have learned to comfort one another at the time of physical death. All these are done because we have come to know that at a time of great loss it is good for people not to be alone. More than anything else, grieving people need to experience the love and concern of their friends and family.

But if the death is that of the marriage relationship, while the pain and grief may be just as real, the family and church and community have no plan of action to comfort and support these individuals. Usually, rather than helping, there is a drawing away because people do not seem to know what to do and say. So at a time when friends who love and care would be most welcome and needed they aren't there.

To complicate matters even further, in the death of a marriage there is no body to bury. The two persons go on living even though their relationship is dead and their presence is a constant reminder of the failure of the marriage. If there are children, though the marriage is over, the family goes on because there are still parents and children (the parents simply no longer live together).

It is difficult for most people to realize the crippling effect a divorce has upon a person. At a wedding reception I overheard a snatch of the conversation between two ladies next to me. They were discussing a young woman from our church who was back home for this particular wedding. The young woman had a distinguished record in college, took a job with a large firm after graduation, and then met and married one of the outstanding young men in the city in which she worked. Three years into the marriage he decided that he didn't love her and wanted out. In spite of strenuous efforts made by every interested party the marriage finally ended in divorce. This was her first trip home following the breakup of her home.

This is what I heard: "It's too bad about her divorce. But she's so young and pretty. She shouldn't have a worry in the world. Why, there are dozens of men who'll be setting their caps for her."

It took more self-control than I normally exhibit to resist telling those dear ladies how wrong they were in sizing up that lovely girl's situation. It is true that she is pretty. But on the inside she does not feel pretty. She feels a sense of failure so intensely that it would be almost impossible for her to describe it.

Right now the last thing in the world she wants is another husband. So hurt and so betrayed does she feel that she is not sure she will ever be able to put herself in the position of being vulnerable again. She feels almost contaminated. Even though she is increasingly afraid of close relationships, she is going to need friends. More than anything else she is coming to doubt her own worth as a person. Her feelings and attitudes are typical of men and women who have experienced the breakdown of a marriage. They may look fairly unscathed from the outside, but inwardly they will have scars from this experience for the rest of their lives.

A man who had learned that our church had done a lot to help the formerly married once asked me, "Aren't you afraid that helping these people will only encourage divorce?" His question told me that he had never been close to anyone who was going through a divorce because it was like asking someone if giving to the American Cancer Fund would make people want cancer. A divorce is a terrible experience.

One night I gave a lecture to over a hundred formerly married men and women and afterwards I spent a period answering the questions which had been written and turned in at the close of my talk. There were questions about guilt and loneliness, grief and fears, children and family. The last question spoke eloquently of what the experience can do to a person. It asked, "What do you do when all you want to do is die, after two years?"

Over the past several years I've seen hundreds who were just as discouraged as that questioner come to a place of new beginning. Because it is a slow process, recovery cannot be rushed. It is not a steady climb for there are so many things which can happen to cause setbacks. And it is not without its anxious moments. A person does not go through such an experience without times of self-doubt and questioning. But when a core of family and friends stand by with steadfast love, and show their concern in little concrete ways, those who face the trauma of divorce can make it.

Such a girl came to us looking years older than her age. She sat on the back row of the seminar on "Beginning Again" and cried all the way through it. Before coming to us, she had already tried all the other places in town to lose her loneliness. But now she was lonelier than ever. I think we must have been her last desperate effort to find help. Talking with her at the recess, I could tell by her defensiveness that she was afraid to relax with us for fear she would be used.

By the fourth week she had found a few friends and had begun to relax. She became involved in a support group which specialized in helping each other through rough times. Though her experiences with the church had left her suspicious, she finally joined a class of seventy-five who were her age and involved in a Sunday morning study. I watched her over more than a year's time. It was like watching a flower open to the sunshine as she responded to the love and support she was receiving.

One day she stopped me as I was going into the building and said, "I don't know if you realized what kind of shape I was in when I came to that first seminar, but I was at the bottom in every way. I may have looked alive but on the inside I was dead to any feeling. What my divorce hadn't done to me I did to myself after the divorce. I know you've been interested in me so I thought you'd like to know. I'm beginning to feel alive again on the inside. And on my good days I even think maybe God has a future for me." Her cure had been love and concern and patience. It's the kind of thing families should do for their members and friends who are in trouble.

Remember the Children

Some of the first divorce laws were designed to offer protection to women who could be divorced for the flimsiest of reasons by the husband simply saying, "I divorce you." But if there is any group which needs protection today it would be the children. Often in the midst of dealing with the divorce we forget them. Because the parents are so important to the children the thought of the parents "not loving each other any more" is almost too much for a child.

I learned something recently from a knowledgable children's worker: often a child gets the feeling that he or she caused the divorce. He may have overheard one of his parents when they were arguing say, "If it weren't for the children I'd get a divorce." The child is not able to understand this completely, but he does put together the emotion of anger and the words "children" and "divorce." He may even feel that something he did or didn't do was responsible. The guilt which a child can accumulate from assuming the responsibility for the breakup of the family can be terribly destructive.

There is no way to predict how a child will react to a divorce and the prospect of not living with both parents. It would depend upon the individual child and the family. Some anxiety can be alleviated if the parents communicate with the children about what is about to happen. Children need to be reassured by their parents that they are loved and will be cared for. They need to be reassured of their worth by the parents. It is sometimes hard for them to grasp the idea that though the marriage is dead the family continues to exist. The adjustment the children have to make is not merely to living with just one parent. It is an adjustment to having two parents who don't live together any more. While this is not easy, with some added effort on the part of both parents and help from friends, the children can have most of their needs met as they grow to adulthood.

There are two major problems which must be dealt with concerning the children, and this can only be done by their parents. First, the parents must make an effort not to let the children become the extended battleground for their own difficulties. It is important for the children to respect and love both parents. This is made difficult when parents ask the child to take sides or share bad stories about the other parent. Some parents even interrogate the child about what was said, done, and observed at the other's house. The natural tendency of those going through a divorce is to divide up the furniture and children. I'm not too worried about the furniture but the children deserve better treatment.

The second problem is to find constructive ways to

meet the needs of the children which were usually met by the absent partner. There's always the tendency, or at least the temptation, on the part of the parent in the home to be overprotective and over-indulgent. The parent who has the children only occasionally is tempted to buy gifts for the children and make all the visits fun and games. Neither of these situations is what the child needs. The needs of children have not changed basically. It's just the means of meeting those needs.

The children of a divorce, both young and old, have the same needs as their parents. They need love and care and assurance. These needs can be met by all the members of the family and extended family plus a host of friends. Don't forget the children. Jesus said, "For the kingdom of God belongs to such as these" (Mark 10:14).

Others Who Help

While the family itself has great potential for healing, when there is a divorce there are others who can help in those areas where the family is limited. A false sense of self-sufficiency can be a dangerous thing and to reach outside for help when it is needed is wise. I've already mentioned (several times) the role of friends. They are almost like extended family and the help they give is similar. I would like to make two other specific suggestions for help.

First, I often send a person whose marriage has failed to a counselor in a marriage and family practice. Though I love people and am interested in them, I do not have the professional training or experience which qualifies me to do the kind of counseling which is needed. The first reaction I always get is, "Kenneth, my divorce is final. There is no hope for reconciliation.

Why a marriage counselor?" Most people only think of professional help while there is some hope of saving the marriage, and even then they usually wait so long to seek help that the counselor is faced with an almost impossible situation.

There is a little analogy I use to explain why they still need help. I ask them to imagine they had been in an accident and one leg had been severed. When someone started to call an ambulance would they raise up and say, "Why call an ambulance since my leg is already gone?" The answer is obvious. We call the ambulance so that in spite of the loss of a limb the person may be saved. The role of the counselor is to help the person sort out all the emotions of what he has been through. The family and friends are needed for support, but the objectivity of the counselor allows one to deal with areas outside the ability of family and friends. I've seen many individuals helped by such counseling. More than one, in evaluating the importance of the experience, has said, "It not only helped me to face what happened in my marriage but helped me lay a foundation for the future."

There are three criteria by which I recommend a counselor. First, he/she must have a Christian viewpoint. This is in contrast to a purely humanistic outlook. The Christian perspective gives an ethical base and an understanding of man's nature and of reality which I think is accurate. Second, I want a counselor with thorough professional training. An increasing number of well qualified men and women are practicing throughout the country. Third, I want a counselor who draws definite boundaries in relationship with his clients. People need a counselor who keeps the relationship entirely on a professional level and does not establish any social or private relationship with the client. These are the kind of people whom God can use to help people.

The second help outside the family I recommend is the church. In the concluding chapter I will be saying a word about new ways in which the church is becoming an ally of the family. In this context let me mention two reasons why I send people who have gone through a divorce to a church.

First, by its very nature the fellowship of the church is geared to meet the needs of the formerly married. One of their big needs is for fellowship without fear of being exploited. Singles clubs and bars make their money by exploiting the loneliness of people—and they profit from sick situations. A friend said to me, "Until someone suggested I ought to go back to church, the only way I could be around people was to join one of these 'Introduction Services' or go to a singles bar. I had forgotten there was the possibility for friendship and companionship without being used." The interesting truth is that the church meets every week, has lots of special meetings, doesn't charge admission, and will take you as you are and accept you and love you.

The second reason I suggest the church is its theology of beginning again. Life has a religious dimension and so does marriage. There is a spiritual meaning to the failure of a marriage. The failure of a marriage is falling short of God's ideal for that relationship. The whole message of the church has to do with how God feels about people who fall short of his ideal in any area of life. He loves them. And because of his own sacrifice through the death of Christ he forgives our wrongs, restores our relationships, and begins working with us where we are to rebuild our lives. People whose marriages have failed are not outside God's love or forgiveness or plans.

Once when Jesus was trying to explain to a legalistic and judgmental group of people what God is like, he told a simple story about a family. He may have observed the family or heard about it. The parable is so well known that its name is a part of the world's vocabulary. It is called "The Prodigal Son." While everyone knows the story, most people have never grasped the real point. It's the story of a man who had two sons. The oldest kept all the rules but was a rebel at heart. The youngest went all the way with his rebellion. He demanded his share of the inheritance, left home, and made one big mess of his life. When he finally came to his senses, he decided to return home, apologize, and ask if he could at least have a position as a hired servant. To his surprise his father came running to meet him, didn't even listen to his explanation, embraced him, received him back as his son, and celebrated his return.

The whole point of the story is to tell how God feels and how God acts toward people who have made messes of their lives. This is the only story the church has and it is true. When a person is trying to survive broken relationships and he feels welcomed and loved in his own family and forgiven and restored in the family of God, then there is hope for the days ahead.

For further thought and discussion:

1. What are things which family and friends can do to augment the experience of children who are living with just one parent?
2. What churches in your city have shown an interest in ministering to the needs of the formerly married?

3. If someone whom you know is going through a divorce, seek out that person and express your concern. Tell him/her you will be thinking about them and will remember to pray for them. Then take time to listen to their response.

4. How would you go about finding a marriage and family counselor to whom you would feel free to go, or to whom you would send your son or daughter?

5. What are some practical things a family could do to communicate love and concern for members who are going through a divorce?

10

Allies for the Family

Since my high school graduation when the class prophet recorded his thoughts on what each of us would be doing ten years later, I've been fascinated by those who try to look into the future and predict what will be happening in certain areas of our lives. This has been especially interesting as it relates to the family.

Some prophets of doom quoting statistics about the number of divorces exceeding the number of marriages suggest that as an institution the family is over the hill and that future generations will have to find some viable alternative to the family. You shouldn't let these folks alarm you too much. They forget that the family is the most durable institution in our society. It is capable of sustaining great shock, living under enormous pressure, and adjusting to all the changes in society without losing its identity as a unit or its effectiveness in meeting needs and transmitting values.

Others so react to the changes that they suggest the family move back to a period in its history when life

was simpler and issues were clearer. Those whose income allows them to buy a farm may be acting out
that wish in their own lives. But once we invented
machines and moved into the cities we set in motion
events which will not be reversed. Many of the changes
in the future will simply be extensions of that move
with the pace accelerated by the invention of the
computer. There *are* implications for the family when
we talk of a society where there is less connection between jobs and income, more money available for
nonessentials, and more and more leisure time. All
this will require adjustments for the family. These
should not be viewed negatively because there are
positive potentials in all that will be happening.

The one thing which will be the same for the family
both today and in the future is that it will always
need allies. The first time I remember seeing the word
"ally" was as a teenager. World War II had just begun
and almost daily there were headlines in the newspaper
that told what the allies were doing. To this day the
word brings to mind a picture of a group of countries
with common goals and common enemies pooling their
resources to help one another. To a degree this is what
families need: people who are as committed as we are
to the idea of the family; people who have resources
which can be addressed to the need; and people who
care and want to help.

The family does not need someone to whom it can
shift the responsibilities of the family. That has probably been done too much already. The family needs
help in equipping itself to do its job. With the com-
plexity of the family plus all the conflicting pressures
of society, it is easy for even the most competent person to admit to himself that he needs some help. There
is so much to know and understand. So many skills

are needed and there seems to be so little time. The wise couple begins to look around in the community for others who are dealing with similar responsibilities whom they could make allies of their family. It is just assumed that in a general way all those institutions in society which help create and maintain order contribute to the family. The schools play an important part in the mental and social development of the children. But the family needs some allies who are more focused and who by their nature are equipped to help families to grow and develop.

Other Families

Not all the needs of a family can be satisfied by information or skills in some area of family life. Sometimes you just need other families who are aware of you and care. This is why keeping in touch with aunts, uncles, cousins, and grandparents is so important. There is great danger to a family when it is isolated from people who know and care. But a family needs more than relatives.

Each time I perform a wedding I have a relaxed session with the bride and groom in which we get acquainted on a more personal level than before. I find out about their families, their interests, and their plans. Eventually we get around to planning the wedding. We decide who will stand where, the order of the service, whether the ushers will take the grandparents out, and all the other details which are a part of the ceremony. Then I give them one bit of advice.

I tell them that I'm very happy to be performing the ceremony but since it lasts only thirty minutes and the marriage is for a lifetime I would like the privilege of helping them with their marriage as well. Here's what I suggest and why:

One of the best things a young couple can do for their marriage is to purposefully develop a relationship with five or six different couples who have similar goals and values and who are interested in building a strong marriage and an effective family. There ought to be enough common interest with each couple that you would enjoy eating at each other's house or apartment, going to sports events together, and sharing many of the experiences of life.

I'm watching this happen now with some of the couples I've married. They help each other when babies come and when there are illnesses. If a parent dies they provide love and comfort. When someone is out of work they are actively concerned. They do everything from complaining about the officials at the basketball game together to sitting together in the recovery waiting room waiting for a biopsy report which could go either way.

What I see them doing is nurturing a relationship with other families and, as a result, weaving a fabric of support for their own. Every family draws strength from every other family. They learn that certain problems for couples are more normal than unique. By being able to pool the knowledge and experiences of everyone they are much more able to solve problems. Just the knowing and caring of other families is a source of strength.

Books! Books! Books!

A book does not make the same kind of an ally as a person, but it does have the potential of giving you insights and understandings which may not be available to you anywhere else.

Though our home had few books when I was small, we had a mother who would read aloud to us and a small public library in the next block. Those books were the only means available to me for expanding my world and I used them. Soon I discovered that the school had a library and the librarian discovered the areas of my developing interests. All sorts of information came to me in books. I'm a firm believer in them.

Normally when we think of books we think of bookstores where they can be purchased. These are good and you might want to buy certain books which you will want to keep for your family. But the best source of books is still the library. If there are none in your community there are lending libraries which check out books by mail. There are probably more libraries in your community than you realize. In addition to public and church libraries there are schools, colleges, universities, and numbers of helping agencies able to advise you on books for the family.

Most libraries are staffed by well-trained people who are delighted to serve you. They will usually take time to point out sections of books on the family, to find specific titles for subjects you're interested in, and even tell you about new books coming in concerning the family. There is hardly any area of interest a mother or father would have but that there is somewhere an understandable and well-written book on the subject.

They Call It Adult Education

While a class, a seminar, or a conference on some phase of family living is not as readily available as a book, such events do have potential for helping you focus on some particular area of interest. They provide an opportunity along with other people to participate in a learning experience.

Such events are usually brief ranging from one session to five or six. Usually they are held at hours con-

Allies for the Family

venient for those who are interested enough to attend. A variety of groups such as churches, schools, helping agencies, and specialists in different areas sponsor such sessions.

Often such educational events are free but on occasions there is a small fee. Subjects discussed may cover all the different aspects of marriage and the family. They will deal with many aspects of parenting and nourishing a marriage. A session under good leadership can be most helpful. Recently I sat in a one-session discussion on the needs of the aging which helped me both to understand aging parents and to think about my own aging process.

The churches have begun to provide many helps for the family. So many events are planned in a six-month period at our church that we have to print a brochure just to list them and give necessary information about them. Parenting conferences, marriage check-up clinics for young couples, conferences for families whose children are grown, sessions for one-parent homes, and a host of other sessions have been offered.

The most interesting series is sponsored by 100 young couples called "Yokemen." They have designed a marriage enrichment dinner-lecture series entitled "Family Affair." Every two months they have dinner together, hear an outstanding speaker on some helpful subject of their choosing, then around coffee and dessert discuss how what they have heard relates to their family. All of these are advertised and are open to people who have no relationship to the church. Many outside individuals take advantage of the dinners.

When you notice a conference, seminar, or special program on something you think would help you to be a better person or mate or parent, call and ask for additional information. It might be something you could work into your schedule which would strengthen your role in the family.

Fellowship of Love

The church I pastor has 7,000 members and its buildings are located just off the downtown area in a transitional community. The location isn't good, the buildings are all old, and the parking situation is desperate. In spite of all these the church is flourishing and membership is growing. Many young families are becoming a part of the church's life. Since there is really no social pressure toward church attendance in a large city, I began to look for the motivation of these families. I discovered that all feel the need for help with their family—and they are finding some of that help in the church. I then began to look at that help from their viewpoint instead of mine and discovered two interesting facts:

First, the families felt support from the fellowship aspect of the church. Most churches have adult Bible study groups. While some insights come from the study, the most significant help they were feeling was the support they received from the group. It met once a week. They were missed if they were absent. Provision was made for their children. There was some social activity involved. Each couple had the chance to meet new and interesting people their own age. It had all the ingredients of support for their family.

The second motive was more subtle but just as real. The couples felt that the key emphases of the church in her historic doctrine were family-centered. The idea of self-esteem was invented by God long before anyone coined the phrase. Early man found his worth from the fact that he reported to God. A basis for relating to other people is mentioned in the summing up of the law. To love God with all your heart and your neighbor as yourself speaks of a loving relationship to self, to others, and to God. Commitment is one of the key ingredients in marriage and the word in the church which is its synonym is "faith." The need to learn how to forgive and be forgiven in the family is the theme of the biblical faith. Notice all the parallels here. We are talking about two kinds of families, the human family and the family of God.

The church also invites you into the kind of personal relationship with God which gives you a sense of unity, direction, and purpose as a person. And as this relationship with God is nourished, you will find that it will help you in every role you play in the family. It has helped me as a father to know that I live in a relationship with a heavenly Father. When I address myself to discipline in the family it is good to remember that I live under a teaching relationship too. When someone in the family has hurt me and I'm finding reconciliation difficult, it helps me to know that One has forgiven me. I feel that God helps me to be a better husband and father than I would be without him.

Its Own Best Friend

Even as you make allies for your family in all the areas I've mentioned, don't forget that a family *can* be its own best friend. All the potential is there waiting to be used. The elements which make for a healthy family are much simpler than most people realize.

Begin with a firm belief in the value of the family. It's the environment where people grow, where creativity is nurtured, where a feeling of safety is experienced, and where self-esteem is developed. Believe in it.

Work at talking with each of the family members

and discovering their good points, things they do well, ideas they have which are good. Stress these instead of the negative. Compliments never go out of style.

Develop the freedom to talk about feelings and learn to be sensitive to the feelings of others. Learn to solve problems creatively and know the good feeling from the accomplishment. When you've done the best you can, you can learn to laugh at the mistakes. And it will make you much more understanding of others when they fail.

The one experience which will give meaning to all the others is:

Love God.
Love yourself.
Love your mate.
Love your children.

When I was a teenager we lived in a rented apartment in a crowded section of town. Carefully I scanned the want ads. The advertisements of new houses for sale interested me most. I had never even known anyone who had lived in a new house. Some of the ads printed floor plans and I studied them as though I had been the architect. Sometimes I would even find myself sitting in a class that wasn't holding my interest making drawings of houses about which I had read in the paper. One day I wrote across the top of one of those drawings: "Someday I am going to have a house." That seemed really to be the desire of my heart, though I don't remember discussing it with anyone.

It was years later before I realized that the deep longing of my boyish heart wasn't for a house but for a home. I have a house now, but the best part of my wish which came true is that there's a family in that house.

My wish for you is that there will be a family in your house too!